beyond
spiritual
gifts

beyond spiritual gifts

rick yohn

TYNDALE HOUSE PUBLISHERS, INC.
Wheaton, Illinois
COVERDALE HOUSE PUBLISHERS, LTD.
Eastbourne, England

Unless they are otherwise identified,
Scripture quotations in this book
are from the New American Standard Bible.

Library of Congress Catalog Card Number 76-5210
ISBN 8423-0112-7, cloth; 8423-0113-5, paper
Copyright © 1976 Tyndale House Publishers, Inc.
Wheaton, Illinois. All rights reserved
First printing, July 1976
Printed in the United States of America

To Linda,

God's choice instrument to teach me how to love
and care for others ... one whose spiritual gifts
and life style are governed by a godly character.

"Her children (Ricky and Steven) stand and bless
her; so does her husband (Rick). He praises her
with these words: 'There are many fine women in
the world, but you are the best of them all' "
(Proverbs 31:28, 29, TLB).

contents

is something missing?

I'd been to Madera once before, but hadn't paid too much attention to directions. Now Keith and I were traveling there for a planning session with three other pastors.

"Don't worry, Keith. Madera is a small town. There's no way we can get lost. The church is right in town." Keith accepted my confidence with a nod and we turned off the freeway to Madera, "Gateway to Yosemite."

Ten minutes passed. "I know it's here somewhere. But just to be safe, I'll pull over to that phone booth and check the address." I thumbed through the yellow pages and found what I was looking for. "Here it is. 119 North R Street." I asked Keith what street we were near.

"We just passed B Street, Rick. Must be down the road."

Forty-five minutes later I pulled up to a fire station and asked directions. According to the fireman, there was no 119 R Street. But when we checked the phone book again that was the address.

I asked to use the phone and called the pastor of our mysteriously misplaced church. He couldn't understand the mix-up but gave me directions to the church.

We got back in the car, and I turned the ignition switch. The car grunted, gasped, and died.

Back to the fire department. Another phone call. This time the other three pastors volunteered to come start my car.

After a cable jump, we followed our rescuers to the church. To my surprise, we were standing a block from where I first stopped to check the yellow pages. The church was located on B Street.

On further investigation we noticed that the print in the Madera phone books was missing something. The bottom part of the line had failed to print. The *R* was actually a *B*.

All that confusion and wasted time—because one section of a letter was missing. A telephone book is supposed to supply useful directory information, but in this case, a poorly printed phone book became a source of misdirection and frustration.

"Misdirection" is a major problem facing Christians. The nature of a Christian by definition is to be like Christ, to live as he would live, to be a "Christ one." Yet frequently, when people examine our lives, they find important qualities missing and they're thrown off the track by what they see.

Think about that person, for instance, who always talks about love and yet shows little love to others. Or the person who uses his spiritual gifts, supposedly for the glory of God, but in a way that seems to glorify himself. Or the woman who speaks of submission to God and yet dominates her husband. Something is lacking in many Christian lives.

Something was missing for years in my own life. I knew that God had given me certain spiritual gifts, so that wasn't the problem. For that matter, he had also provided years of education and experience to develop them. But in spite of the discovery, development, and use of these gifts, I continued to experience repeated periods of moodiness, temper, impatience, anger.

Only within the past two years have I begun to focus on my real need: character development. The effectiveness of my gifts had increased, but not the maturity of my character. I was able to tell others to be more Christlike, but I failed to show them how. I personally needed to develop "his likeness." Without maturity of character, I was only going through the motions of seeking spiritual growth, a problem that has plagued Christians since the first believers in Antioch became known as Christians.

GIFTS WITHOUT MATURING CHARACTER: FIRST-CENTURY PROBLEM

The Corinthian church was a case in point. They lacked none of the gifts (1 Corinthians 1:4, 5, 7a). The church had apostles, prophets, teachers, miracles, gifts of healings, helps, administrations, various kinds of tongues (12:28). Yet in spite of their spiritual gifts, they were plagued by self-inflicted problems. They didn't exhibit beautiful lives. They lacked mature spiritual character.

The Corinthian church was known for being divisive (1:11-13), jealous, argumentative (3:3), and immoral (5:1, 2); they defrauded one another (6:1-8); they abused their freedom in Christ (8, 9); they were stingy and got drunk during their love feasts (11:20-22); they tended to elevate the gift of tongues above other gifts (12, 14); and some of them were doubting the validity of Christ's resurrection (15:12).

What was the underlying problem in that church? The Apostle Paul pierced through their facade and exposed the real issue: they had failed to develop mature spiritual character. Therefore, they often had no adequate spiritual means to govern interpersonal relationships, activities within Corinthian society, or the development and use of their spiritual gifts (3:1). They had neglected that "more excellent way."

"But earnestly desire the greater gifts. And I show you a still more excellent way. If I speak with the tongues of men and of angels, *but do not have love,* I have become a noisy gong or a clanging cymbal. And if I have the gift of prophecy, and know all mysteries and all knowledge; and if I have all faith, so as to remove mountains, *but do not have love,* I am nothing. And if I give all my possessions to feed the poor, and if I deliver my body to be burned, *but do not have love,* it profits me nothing" (12:21—13:3).

As Christians the Corinthians had been united with God through faith in Jesus Christ. The Holy Spirit was indwelling them so that they each possessed the nature of God through the person of the Holy Spirit. Therefore they each had great potential for spiritual development. Yet this development had not progressed far enough. Their spiritual gifts needed to be governed and enhanced by character, especially love. However, the manifestation of their spiritual gifts had become the principal focus for their lives rather than this loving character.

DEFINING TERMS

A spiritual gift is an ability given to any believer so that he or she may accomplish the will of God. We all possess at least one God-given ability, perhaps several. Some of the spiritual gifts are specified in Romans 12:6-8, 1 Corinthians 12—14, Ephesians 4:11, and 1 Peter 4:10, 11. In my book *Discover Your Spiritual Gift and Use It* (Wheaton, Illinois: Tyndale House Publishers, 1974, pp. 128-130), I categorize twenty gifts in the Scriptures.

ministry of helping

1. Serving—the ability to give assistance or aid in any way that brings strength or encouragement to others.
2. Giving—the ability to make and distribute money to further the cause of God.
3. Showing mercy—the ability to work joyfully with those whom the majority ignores.
4. Craftsmanship—the ability to work with one's hands for the benefit of others.
5. Healings—the ability to heal a person spiritually, emotionally, or physically.

ministry of directing others

1. Leadership (administration)—the ability to lead others and manage the affairs of the church.
2. Faith—the ability to trust God beyond the probable and raise the vision of others.

ministry of the Word

These gifts have a direct relation with the Scriptures.

1. Apostleship—the ability to begin a new work for the Lord through the ministry of the Word.
2. Prophecy—the ability to proclaim or preach God's Word.
3. Evangelism—the ability to present Christ in such a way that people usually respond by faith.
4. Pastor-Teacher—the ability to care for people's spiritual needs through teaching the Word of God. The ability to nurture others in truth.
5. Teaching—the ability to analyze and interpret God's truth and communicate it clearly and systematically.
6. Exhortation—the ability to motivate people to action, normally using the authority of God's Word.
7. Wisdom—the ability to apply God's truth to life.
8. Knowledge—the ability to know truth by the impression of the Holy Spirit.
9. Discernment of spirits—the ability to discern the spirits of truth and error.
10. Music—the ability to express one's relationship to God through music.

ministry of the spectacular

(I wasn't sure how to categorize the final three gifts. Since they often call attention to themselves, I use the term *spectacular*.)

1. Miracles—the ability to perform acts apparently contrary to natural laws, with power beyond human capacity.
2. Tongues—the ability to speak in a language unlearned by the speaker.
3. Interpretation—the ability to interpret the meaning of a tongue, though the interpreter hasn't learned the language.

As you went through this list, one or several of the gifts may have struck a familiar chord. But if you are still in the dark about your particular gift, read on. The gifts are illustrated throughout this book. You may run into an old friend.

Spiritual character, on the other hand, is manifested in the development and consistent practice of life qualities that flow out of our relationship with God: "Christ in you" (Colossians 1:27). The Apostle John referred to spiritual character as God's seed abiding in you (1 John 3:9). Peter referred to it when mentioning certain qualities in the believer's life: "Applying all diligence, in your faith supply moral excellence, and in your moral excellence, knowledge; and in your knowledge, self-control; and in your self-control, perseverance; and in your perseverance, godliness; and in your godliness, brotherly kindness; and in your brotherly kindness, Christian love" (2 Peter 1:5-7). Then notice what he said about the result of developing these qualities in our lives. "For if these qualities are yours and are increasing, they render you neither useless nor unfruitful in the true knowledge of our Lord Jesus Christ" (2 Peter 1:8).

Paul provided several descriptions of spiritual character. He spoke of "the new self" and "the fruit of the Spirit." "Do not lie to one another, since you laid aside the old self with its evil practices, and have put on the new self ... And so ... put on a heart of compassion, kindness, humility, gentleness and patience; bearing with one another, and forgiving each other ... And beyond all these things put on love" (Colossians 3:9-12). "But the fruit of the Spirit is love, joy, peace, patience, kindness, goodness, faithfulness, gentleness, self-control" (Galatians 5:22, 23).

In summary, we can conclude that spiritual character is God's character. It stems from God's nature. When a person receives Christ, he receives this character through the presence of the Holy Spirit who comes to live in his life. The Christian then has potential power to live the life God intended for him. Now notice what happens when believers develop spiritual character and let it govern their spiritual gifts.

GIFTS GOVERNED BY MATURING CHARACTER: FIRST-CENTURY REALITY

When persecution broke out upon the Christians in Jerusalem, many of them scattered to other parts of Judea. Others went beyond that province into Asia Minor. A church was established in the city of Antioch. When news reached Jerusalem that the Gentiles in Antioch had turned to Christ, Barnabas was sent to encourage them. Barnabas had the gift of exhortation, the ability to help others by motivating them to action. He challenged, encouraged, and rebuked.

But Barnabas was known not only for his gifts. The historian Luke completed the account by adding, "For he was a good man, and full of the Holy Spirit and of faith." Barnabas was known in the Christian community as a man whose character and gifts were complementary. The results? "And considerable numbers were brought to the Lord" (Acts 11:24).

Examining the life of another first-century Christian, we notice a similar complementary relationship. It was said of Stephen that he was a man "full of grace and power." Luke described his gift of miracles: "performing great wonders and signs among the people" (Acts 6:8). Stephen also used his gift of prophecy to preach Christ to the Jewish leaders. The result of this confrontation was his public execution. As he lay dying, Stephen's godly character was revealed when he cried out, "Lord, do not hold this sin against them!" (Acts 7:60). Little did Stephen realize the impression he was making on a young man named Saul (7:58).

Philip was another early Christian whose character governed his gifts, resulting in great works for God. Philip possessed the gifts of prophecy (Acts 8:5), evangelism (8:12; 21:8), and the working of miracles (8:6). When he was first chosen to be a deacon, no mention was made of these gifts. The decision was made on the basis of his godly character. " 'But select from among you, brethren, seven men of good reputation, full of the Spirit and of wisdom' ... and they chose ... Philip" (6:3, 5). The results of Philip's character and gifts working together were described in Acts 8:12. "But when they believed Philip preaching the good news about the kingdom of God and the name of Jesus Christ, they were being baptized, men and women alike."

GIFTS GOVERNED BY MATURING CHARACTER: PRESENT REALITY

This quality of life style is not limited to saints of the first century. God wants you to experience a growing, meaningful life as you develop a godly character. In turn this will affect and control the use of your spiritual gifts.

I have a friend who teaches at the California State University of Fresno. He happens to be an excellent teacher. But his students see far more than a man who uses good teaching techniques. They sense genuine love in their professor. They are treated as individuals with potential to develop, not as numbers on a computer card. They are aware of his personal relationship with Jesus Christ and respect him for it. Even his faculty friends recognize the uniqueness of his godly character.

Another friend uses her gift of exhortation to help unwed mothers. Many Christians would spend their time pointing an accusing finger at these young women, but this person loves them into the kingdom of Christ. She spends hours listening, comforting, encouraging, advising, and praying with them. At times she is yelled at, sometimes even threatened. But as her love controls her gift, these young mothers often repent of their confused lives and turn to Christ.

Another friend enjoys using his gift of helping to relieve the frustrations of those who, like myself, aren't handy at fixing things. One of our church members needed a steel fence around his backyard to protect his children from a nearby pool. My friend spent an afternoon installing the fence. Recently one of my lawn sprinklers broke off. (Many homes in Fresno have sprinkling systems because of the arid climate.) I spent several frustrating hours attempting to remove the broken end from the pipe. I mentioned the problem to my friend. The next evening he remedied the situation within minutes, not grudgingly but with genuine Christian love.

GIFTS GOVERNED BY MATURING CHARACTER: YOURS?

How about you? You are a spiritually gifted person, if Jesus Christ is your Savior (1 Corinthians 12:11). You also possess God's character through the person of the Holy Spirit (2 Corinthians 5:17). But when people are exposed to you, do they sense him? Do they realize that Christ really does live in you? Are others blessed and drawn closer to the Lord because of you?

I sincerely hope so. Without a maturing spiritual character, our spiritual gifts are of little value.

spiritual character

"And God made the two great lights, the greater light to govern the day, and the lesser light to govern the night" (Genesis 1:16). Both the sun and the moon are essential to mankind, yet one is greater than the other. Each provides light. But one generates light while the other reflects it.

God has given two kinds of ability to the church. He has provided the potential for godly character which enables a believer to *be*. He has also distributed spiritual gifts which enable a believer to *do*. Both abilities are essential for the health of the Body, although *being* is more important than doing. "But earnestly desire the greater gifts. And I show you a still more excellent way" (1 Corinthians 12:31). Sandwiched in between Paul's discussion of various gifts (1 Corinthians 12) and the special gift of prophecy (chapter 14) lies his description of the more excellent way (chapter 13).

Here Paul summed up the character of God in one overpowering quality: *love*. He was not minimizing the value of spiritual gifts. Earlier he wrote that they have been given for the common good (12:7), though in comparison with spiritual character, gifts have the lesser value.

"But what if I possess the gifts of tongues and prophecy, or the gifts of wisdom and knowledge, or the gifts of faith and giving? Aren't spiritual gifts all I need for effective service?" Absolutely not! Without love, gifts produce little spiritual value (1 Corinthi-

19

ans 13:1-3). They are of benefit only when integrated with spiritual character.

A local church can exist without all of the gifts. But problems abound when it is deficient in love, joy, peace, patience, kindness, goodness, faithfulness, gentleness, and self-control.

CHARACTER IS PREREQUISITE FOR SPIRITUAL LEADERSHIP

When a church seeks spiritual leadership it usually looks for gifted teachers, administrators, and leaders. But how many churches have split because of a dominant leader, dogmatic teacher, or perfectionist administrator? Certainly it would be foolish not to consider a person's gift when a church looks for leadership, but the search must go beyond that. Consider the following New Testament examples.

The Apostle Paul listed fifteen qualifications for the elders of the church. Of the fifteen, only one ("able to teach") could be considered a spiritual gift: "above reproach, the husband of one wife, temperate, prudent, respectable, hospitable, able to teach, not addicted to wine or pugnacious, but gentle, uncontentious, free from the love of money. He must be one who manages his own household well, keeping his children under control with all dignity ... and not a new convert ... and he must have a good reputation with those outside the church" (1 Timothy 3:2-7).

The first deacons were selected primarily on the basis of character. "But select from among you, brethren, seven men of good reputation, full of the Spirit and of wisdom, whom we may put in charge of this task" (Acts 6:3). The apostles were more concerned about a leader's reputation than his gift. They wanted to be certain that the individual was controlled by the One who imparts spiritual gifts.

Further, of the eight qualifications for deacons, none could be considered spiritual gifts. "Deacons likewise must be men of dignity, not double-tongued, or addicted to much wine or fond of sordid gain, but holding to the mystery of faith with a clean conscience. And let these also first be tested; then let them serve if they are beyond reproach ... let deacons be husbands of only one wife, and good managers of their children and their own households" (1 Timothy 3:8-10, 12, 13).

And whether or not you interpret the women in 1 Timothy 3 as deacons' wives or as deaconesses, their qualifications also emphasized character. "Women must likewise be dignified, not malicious gossips, but temperate, faithful in all things" (1 Timothy 3:11).

CHARACTER DETERMINES DISCIPLESHIP

Though the disciples performed miracles and cast out demons, Jesus did not emphasize these abilities as distinguishing marks of discipleship. On several occasions, he aligned discipleship with spiritual character.

A disciple is *loving.* "By this all men will know that you are My disciples, if you have love for one another" (John 13:35). When Jesus spoke these words, his disciples were more divisive than loving. Can you imagine them arguing about who would be greatest in the kingdom (Mark 9:33, 34; Luke 22:24)?

A disciple is *obedient.* "Jesus therefore was saying to those Jews who had believed Him, 'If you abide in My word, then you are truly disciples of Mine' " (John 8:31). To abide in Jesus' word means to remain in it. As his Word saturates your mind and motivates your heart, you demonstrate discipleship.

A disciple is *fruitful.* How productive is your spiritual life? Jesus said, "By this is My Father glorified, that you bear much fruit, and so prove to be My disciples" (John 15:8). Do you see spiritual fruit when you use your gift of teaching? Helping? Showing mercy? Giving? Faith? Craftsmanship? Music? Are people blessed? Is God effecting spiritual change in the lives of others as you employ your gift?

A disciple is *totally committed to Jesus.* The Lord taught, "If anyone comes to Me and does not hate [by comparison with his love for Christ] his own father and mother and wife and children and brothers and sisters, yes, and even his own life, he cannot be My disciple" (Luke 14:26, 27). We could add to this list, "And

[hate] his own spiritual gift." Our gifts must be placed at his disposal, if we want to be Jesus' disciples. "Lord, here is my gift of leadership (tongues, prophecy, exhortation ...). Use this gift for your glory. Build up other believers with it. Help others to see that I am your disciple by my total commitment to you. May they know that you are the most important Person of my life. May they be aware that I've placed you above my family, gifts, ambition, and everything else I possess and hope to achieve."

Spiritual gifts are essential to serving the Lord in specific ministries. But *spiritual character must control those gifts*. Discipleship is determined by our love, obedience, faithfulness, and commitment to Jesus Christ.

CHARACTER PRODUCES POSITIVE SPIRITUAL RESULTS

When the Holy Spirit distributed his gifts, he desired them to be used in a positive way. But even in the early church, gifts were at times used for selfish purposes with negative results. Knowledge produced pride (1 Corinthians 8:1). Tongues brought confusion (14:23, 26-33, 40). Prophecy and teaching produced divisions (3:4-9). Such undesirable results were not always the fault of the one who possessed the gift (3:4-9).

On the other hand, spiritual character produces positive results. "Love is patient, love is kind, and is not jealous; love does not brag and is not arrogant, does not act unbecomingly; it does not seek its own, is not provoked, does not take into account a wrong suffered, does not rejoice in unrighteousness, but rejoices with the truth; bears all things, believes all things, hopes all things, endures all things. Love never fails" (13:4-8a).

Suppose God has given you a beautiful voice. As you sing his praises, people are blessed. But a visitor with a critical spirit sits in the congregation. As she listens to you sing, she thinks, "What a showoff. Look at her. That phony smile." After the service, you providentially meet this visitor. With genuine love and kindness you welcome her to the church. As you chat, the woman's critical spirit begins to melt. She senses that you aren't a phony. Your love and concern for her are genuine. She wants to return next week, because in the space of a few moments, her critical spirit is changed.

CHARACTER FULFILLS THE BASIC COMMANDS OF SCRIPTURE

Ever hear someone say, "Oh, I'd love to help—but that just isn't my gift"? What we fail to realize is that many ministries can be accomplished by *every* believer, whatever his or her gift. Spiritual gifts are special abilities given for specific responsibilities. If I have the gift of teaching, I should seek opportunities to teach. A special gift for a specialized ministry. With God's character, however, you are equipped to perform many tasks. The following list of commands can be accomplished by developing and using your spiritual character, no matter what gift you have.

Love one another (Romans 12:9).
Concern yourself with others and honor them (12:10).
Pray for others (12:12).
Share your material possessions with others (12:13).
Be hospitable to others (12:13).
Maintain the unity of the Body (12:16).
Build up others spiritually (14:19; 15:2).
Accept others for what they are (15:7).
Admonish others (15:14).
Serve others (Galatians 5:13).
Bear the burdens of others (Galatians 6:2).
Be patient (Ephesians 4:2).
Be kind and forgiving (Ephesians 4:32).
Comfort others (1 Thessalonians 4:18).
Encourage others (Hebrews 3:13; 10:23-25).
Confess your sins (James 5:16).

You are both a specialist and a general practitioner. You are capable of accomplishing each of these tasks because God's character is within you. You've been equipped to fulfill a special service because God has given you at least one spiritual gift. So, go to it. Do the "work of service" as God opens opportunities for you. Spiritual gifts, governed by maturing spiritual character, are sufficient resource.

what is this thing called love?

A seventeen-year-old sobs to her counselor in an unwed mothers' home. "But he said he loved me. I don't sleep around. I've been brought up in a good Christian home. I love my parents. And I love Tom. That's why this happened. But Tom doesn't want to marry me. Not now!"

In another section of town, Art and Mary are having their daily early-morning ritual.

Art: "Must we go through that again? I told you a hundred times. I've got to work late at night. We have to get those accounts finished by the end of the week."

Mary: "But it's not just this week. It's every week and every night. Why can't you come home at six like Sally's husband? He's always home by then. Sometimes I wonder if you really love me."

Art: "Don't start that again!"

Mary: "But what am I supposed to think? Monday it was eight o'clock. Tuesday, nine-thirty. And last night..."

Art: "Look, Mary, I'm telling you for the last time. I could have married a dozen girls. But I chose you. Now get off my back! I told you when we got married I loved you. How often does a guy have to repeat it?"

That same day, Jim Meyers is in his pastor's office seeking advice. "Pastor, I don't know what's been bugging me lately. I can't sleep at night. I can't keep my mind on my work during the day. I've searched my heart and I can't think of any gross sin I've committed. I just don't know what's wrong. I'm not even sure why I came in to talk with you."

"Well, Jim, I don't have any magic formula that's going to solve your problem. But I've noticed that you and Al haven't been talking with each other lately."

"Pastor, leave Al out of the conversation. I can't stand that guy. We used to be the best of friends. But after what he did to me I'll never forgive him. And don't bother quoting that "love your neighbor" jazz. No way, could I possibly love *him*....."

Love. One of those four-letter words that means almost anything people want it to mean. A man may say, "I love golf; I love shrimp; I love my wife," all in the same breath. Is it possible that neither the seventeen-year-old nor Art nor Jim knows what love is? Is it possible that their love is extremely immature?

When I was in seminary we bought a beagle pup. Since we had no children at the time we poured our parental love into our dog, Snoopy. She spent most of her waking hours in the house. She enjoyed sleeping in our bed and on our furniture. She was our companion when we traveled from Dallas to Pennsylvania. She moved with us to Minneapolis and continued to be treated like a child. But on November 20, 1964, Snoopy's life style began to change.

Our first son was born that day. And though my wife and I loved "man's best friend," we soon discovered that there are degrees of love. Time, conversation, thoughts, and emotions were now wrapped up in our son. Snoopy was still petted, fed, and played with, but love had found a new dimension, a new object.

What is love? One popular view promotes love solely as an emotion to be expressed in a sexual relationship. Some film-makers, song writers, and authors go to great lengths to sell this concept.

Others see love as that warm feeling you get when someone is very close to you physically, emotionally, or even spiritually.

The Greeks referred to four types of love. They spoke of a sexual love: *eros*. Though the word *eros* is not found in the New Testament, it is illustrated in the Old Testament story of the relationship between Amnon and his half sister, Tamar. After conniving to be alone with her, Amnon forcéd Tamar into a sexual relationship. The result was a strong sense of guilt which led to hate. "Then Amnon hated her with a very great hatred; for the hatred with which he hated her was greater than the love with which he had loved her" (2 Samuel 13:15). *Eros* is the sensual kind of love that lasts only as long as its object remains appealing.

A second kind of love, *storge,* would describe what my wife and I expressed to our beagle—natural love. Paul called it "natural affection" (Romans 1:31). Hitler had this kind of love for music. People direct this love toward flowers, art, hobbies, etc.

Another word used by the Greeks to describe love was *phileo.* The city's name Philadelphia ("brotherly love") is derived from this word. A philanthropist is a "lover of mankind." The concept portrayed by *phileo* was "friendship." At times this word was used as an emotional affection and was close to the term *eros.* But normally it demonstrated a greater maturity of love.

A fourth level of love, *agape,* included the emotions but wasn't limited by them. It included a natural affection, but even when it wasn't natural to love, *agape* loved anyway. This love provided an excellent basis for companionship, but it transcended that phase if the companion failed to love in return.

When the Bible states that God is love, it uses *agape.* John wrote, "God so loved [*agape*] the world, that He gave His only begotten Son" (John 3:16). *Agape* gives. *Agape* sacrifices. *Agape* initiates love. "We love, because He first loved us" (1 John 4:19). The child doesn't love its mother at birth, but the mother loves her child. Then as the mother continues to show her child love during the weeks, months, and years, the child learns to love its mother.

Agape loves whether or not the object deserves that love. "But God demonstrates His own love toward us, in that while we were yet sinners, Christ died for us" (Romans 4:8).

A husband who loves his wife as Christ loved [*agape*] the church will make every sacrifice to meet her needs (not necessarily all her wants). He will provide for her physical needs of sexual love, financial security, clothes, food, etc. He will provide for her emotional needs like security, affection, understanding, acceptance, the feeling of being wanted, and of feeling necessary to complete him. He will provide for her spiritual needs by encouraging her to grow in the Lord. He will set the example of what it means to walk in the Spirit.

This love is the culmination of the other three. It is a love arising from maturity. It is a love that gives itself for the benefit of others and for the glory of God. It is consistent with God's will. It is costly.

TO LOVE IS COSTLY

Salvation is free to the sinner, but provision for salvation was costly. God had one Son, and he gave him to die for us. It cost God to love, and it will cost us to love.

Recently I asked a father if he loved his children. His reply was immediate. "Certainly I love them. What kind of father would I be if I didn't?"

"That's interesting," I said. "Your son hasn't gotten the message."

The father replied, "But I've given him everything he wants. When he was a young boy he got the best bike money could buy. Then I bought him a new Honda. For his sixteenth birthday he received a new car. What else does he need?"

"He needs your *time*," I replied. This well-meaning father was so busy being successful in his company that he had no time left for his family.

But time isn't the only price we must pay to love. *Privacy* is another cost factor. Many of us like to guard our privacy as though it were Fort Knox. But there are times when we cannot simultaneously maintain love and privacy. A case in point is recorded in Mark's Gospel.

Jesus and his disciples had put in a full day's work teaching and healing. He and the disciples were tired and hungry, but the people remained. Finally Jesus told his disciples to come with him, away from the crowd, to a quiet place. They would find rest and refreshment. They got into a boat and headed toward a lonely place across the lake. But as they sailed, the people ran around the shoreline, forming a welcoming committee as they disembarked.

Though in need of privacy, Jesus had compassion on the multitude and began to teach them. The hour grew late. The weary disciples interrupted the Lord. "The place is desolate and it is already quite late; send them away so that they may go into the surrounding countryside and villages and buy themselves something to eat" (Mark 6:35, 36).

At first glance that might not look so bad, to be interested in people's needs. But if you read between the lines, the disciples were probably saying, "Lord, we've had it! Get rid of these people so we can get some food and rest!"

The disciples wanted their privacy. The multitude was invading it. Ever feel like that? You're tired. You've had a hard day. Then the phone rings. Someone needs help. You're asked to come over immediately. Your privacy has been invaded. You must choose between an act of love and an act of selfishness. The choice isn't easy. Love may cost you some privacy.

Love can also be *expensive materially.* Suppose you have new wall-to-wall carpeting in your living room. The youth sponsor in your church asks to hold a Bible study at your house—for thirty high school kids. You cringe because last year's Bible study is still fresh in your memory. During the year refreshments were served a few times. Two "sloppy Joes" and three glasses of grape punch were spilled on the old carpet. Do you dare take another chance? That all depends on the price you're willing to pay to reach young people for Christ.

It may be gas for transportation, money for the church budget and special projects, a living room carpet, a favorite record album, a tape recorder, and a hundred and one other material things. Whatever the item, it may get abused, broken, smashed, stained, charred, riddled, chipped, ruined, or stolen. You have to decide about your value system. As long as you value things more than people, you'll be tempted to refuse the use of your things. But if you value people above things, you'll generally take the risk of damage and loss. Jesus' commentary on the divine value system was recorded by Matthew: "Do not lay up for yourselves treasures upon earth, where moth and rust destroy, and where thieves break in and steal. But lay up for yourselves treasures in heaven, where neither moth nor rust destroys, and where thieves do not break in or steal; for where your treasure is, there will your heart be also" (Matthew 6:19-21).

Time, privacy, material goods. They may have to be sacrificed when we love others. But one further price is that little four-letter word *work*. To love another isn't always convenient. Love isn't a part-time job. It's demanding, tiresome, at times just hard work.

The Apostle Paul described the "price he paid to love the ungodly": "... in far more labors, in far more imprisonments, beaten times without number, often in danger of death. Five times I received from the Jews thirty-nine lashes. Three times I was beaten with rods, once I was stoned, three times I was shipwrecked, a night and a day I have spent in the deep. I have been on frequent journeys, in dangers from rivers, dangers from robbers, dangers from my countrymen, dangers from the Gentiles, dangers in the city, dangers in the wilderness, dangers on the sea, dangers among false brethren; I have been in labor and hardship, through many sleepless nights, in hunger and thirst, often without food, in cold and exposure. Apart from such external things, there is the daily pressure upon me of concern for all the churches. Who is weak without my being weak?" (2 Corinthians 11:23-29a).

God may never call you or me to experience such hardship. But he will expect us to express our love in service—and that takes work. "For you were called to freedom, brethren; only do not turn your freedom into an opportunity for the flesh, but *through love serve one another*" (Galatians 5:13).

NOT TO LOVE IS MORE COSTLY

When love is withheld from members of the local church, that congregation may pay the price of disunity (1 Corinthians 1:10-17; 2:4-9), immaturity (1 Corinthians 3:1, 2), jealousy and strife (1 Corinthians 3:3), favoritism (James 2:1-10), indifference

(James 2:14-16; 1 John 3:16-18), and lack of care for one another (Romans 14:15).

When love is withheld from the family the results will be anger (Ephesians 6:4), insecurity in the lives of the children and spouse (Colossians 3:21), and unanswered prayer for the husband and wife (1 Peter 3:7).

When love is withheld from relationships with others, your personal life pays a high price. You may become enslaved to those you dislike. I knew someone who despised his father. He determined as a young man that he would never become hateful like his father, yet in spite of this, the more hateful he became. His bitterness became his master.

Withhold love from others, and your spiritual life is immediately affected. You lose the joy of your salvation. Fellowship with God is broken. Your emotional life is thrown out of whack. You become tense and irritable. You refuse to forgive, and that bothers your conscience because you know that God has forgiven you of worse sins. Eventually, you may leave some doctor's office with the diagnosis that you have an ulcer. What began with a decision not to love affects your spiritual, emotional, mental, and physical life.

Love is always costly. But to withhold love is to pay an unnecessary and eventually overburdening price.

THE REWARDS OF LOVE

Love has rewards. One is that love *begets love*. The Apostle John wrote, "We love, because He first loved us" (1 John 4:19). Whom do we love because of his love? We love God and we love one another. "Beloved, if God so loved us, we also ought to love one another" (1 John 4:11). Jesus Christ is the example of how husbands should love their wives (Ephesians 5:25). It's extremely difficult to hate someone who loves you. It's not impossible, but you really have to work at it.

Just as natural love can be learned in the home, Christian love can be learned in the family of God. Enter a congregation where love among the brethren is obvious and you find it easy to love in return. But enter a church where there is friction, division, and bitterness. Your love does not flow as freely.

Love also develops a sense of security. "There is no fear in love; but perfect love casts out fear" (1 John 4:18). Security is normally developed in the home. Dr. Tim LaHaye writes: "A parent's love is more important to a child than wealth or education or any form of material possession. When a child basks in the security of his parents' love he gradually develops a wholesome outlook toward life. The home can fall far short of perfection in many areas; this lack will serve to prepare the child for life in an imperfect world. But the one thing he must have for a positive mental attitude is love" *(How To Be Happy Though Married,* Wheaton, Illinois: Tyndale House Publishers, 1968, p. 79).

The parents' love will help a child accept authority without fear. A mother's love will help a son relate properly to women without fear. A father's love will help insure a daughter's healthy relationship with men later in life. Again, Dr. LaHaye writes: "Since her first masculine image is her father she is prone to transfer this image to all men, including her husband. Whatever resentment and hostility she had been fostering in her heart against her father is often transferred to her husband" (p. 82).

People who are unsure of themselves and who maintain a low self-image are often the products of a love-starved family background. They lack personal security and they find it difficult to love another individual deeply.

Love pays further dividends in our spiritual life. It *confirms spiritual realities.* In his Gospel and epistles, John presents four spiritual experiences that are proven to be true when love is expressed.

(1) The individual who consistently loves proves his personal relationship with Jesus Christ. "Beloved, let us love one another, for love is from God; and every one who loves is born of God and knows God. The one who does not love does not know God, for God is love" (1 John 4:7, 8).

(2) The consistent lover of people proves his love for God. "If someone says, 'I love God,' and hates his brother, he is a liar; for the one who does not love his brother whom he has seen, cannot

love God whom he has not seen" (1 John 4:20). How hypocriti-
cal of two feuding people in a local church at eleven A.M. Sunday
to be singing, "Oh, how I love Jesus."

(3) A loving person demonstrates that he is a disciple of Christ.
Jesus said, "By this all men will know that you are My disciples,
if you have love for one another" (John 13:35). Some Christians
think that discipleship is tested by how many verses they
memorize. Others rate discipleship on the basis of things they
don't do. Some determine discipleship by the number of commit-
tees they chair and the number of services they attend. Jesus said
that discipleship is directly related to the love we have for others.

(4) A loving individual is in fellowship with God. "The one
who says he is in the light [walking in fellowship] and yet hates
his brother is in the darkness until now. The one who loves his
brother abides in the light and there is no cause for stumbling in
him. But the one who hates his brother is in darkness and walks
in the darkness, and does not know where he is going because
the darkness has blinded his eyes" (1 John 2:9-11).

A number of years ago I was a youth speaker at a fall retreat in
Canada. After the first evening of games, singing, speaking, and
counseling, I went to my bedroom in a state of exhaustion. As I
hit the bed I fell asleep. But about two A.M. I heard a loud clanging outside. It sounded as if someone was throwing around garbage can lids. In the darkness I felt my way toward the window
and looked out. There was enough moonlight to recognize the
culprit, a bear. Since this was my first exposure to a real live bear
within a few feet of where I stood, I decided to watch the action.

Eventually I groped my way back to fall on what I thought was
my bed. I missed the bed completely and landed flat on the floor.
The wind was knocked out of me. I was certain the bed had been
there moments before. But I was walking in darkness, not knowing where I was going.

You may think you're walking in fellowship with God because
you attend church, or because you don't swear. But the Bible
says that you actually are walking in darkness unawares if you
are embittered against a fellow believer. In that case you'll experience two certainties: stumbling around in life and getting
hurt.

What is this thing called love? It is a *self-giving attitude toward God and man* that is costly but rewarding. How can you experience this love and show it to others? Read on.

how can I love?

Many of our tests of spirituality fall short of biblical example. For instance, there is the "I don't do that" syndrome. Most of the prohibitions center around drinking, smoking, movies, dancing, card playing, and "Sabbath" keeping. The underlying principle of this philosophy is, If you don't do these things you're spiritual. If you do any of them, you're unspiritual. Many Christians become known in their communities for what they don't do.

Without advocating that we go out and indulge, I want to convey an important biblical observation. Jesus was known in his community for what he did:

he healed the sick
raised the dead
fed the 5,000
cleansed the temple
turned water to wine
walked on water
gave sight to the blind
preached the kingdom of God
regularly attended services in the synagogue and temple
taught with authority
prayed to his Father
had compassion on the multitudes
contended with the traditionalism of the Pharisees and the liberalism of the Sadducees.

God is love. Love is active. Jesus loved by healing, preaching, teaching, contending, serving, and praying. Love usually isn't demonstrated by living in isolation. Love is developed and expressed by interacting with people. This chapter offers some suggestions about how you can express *agape* love.

LOVE DOES WHAT IS GOOD

We love by doing whatever is good for others. For example, when I see another Christian wrestling with a sinful habit, I have a choice to make. If I'm comparing my spiritual life with his, I can choose to judge him and pat myself on the back for avoiding that sin. If I love him, I'll choose to make myself available to help him in his struggle. "Brethren, even if a man is caught in any trespass, you who are spiritual, restore such a one in a spirit of gentleness; looking to yourselves, lest you too be tempted" (Galatians 6:1).

Further, if a friend has a problem and tries to share it with me, I have a choice. If I'm bothered about my own problems, I can interrupt and tell him, "Everything will work out OK. You'll see. Just trust God." But if I love him, I'll choose to listen to the problem. I may share some possible solutions. I'll pray with him and continue to support him until the problem is solved. "Bear one another's burdens, and thus fulfill the law of Christ" (Galatians 6:2).

On the other hand, if the need is physical, then love will supply it to the best of its ability. John warned about loving in word rather than in action. "But whoever has the world's goods, and beholds his brother in need and closes his heart against him, how does the love of God abide in him? Little children, let us not love with word or with tongue, but in deed and truth" (1 John 3:17, 18).

It's exciting for me to pastor a church whose young people constantly express love for our sick and shut-in by deed. They clean their houses. They mow their lawns. They do whatever needs to be done. It's their way of saying "We love you."

LOVE ACTS WITHIN GOD'S WILL

We express *agape* love when we meet needs in a way that is consistent with God's will and character. One day a young lawyer came to Jesus. Approaching the Lord, he said, "Teacher, which is the great commandment in the Law?" Jesus replied, "You shall love the Lord your God with all your heart, and with all your soul, and with all your mind. This is the great and foremost commandment" (Matthew 22:36, 37). Jesus didn't say that to love was the greatest commandment. He specifically stated that to love God was the greatest. Then he declared another commandment. "And a second is like it. 'You shall love your neighbor as yourself.' On these two commandments depend the whole Law and the Prophets [the rest of the Old Testament]."

Today society has confused the issue. Popular singers cry out, "What the World Needs Now Is Love, Sweet Love." But they're singing about a love that doesn't have to conform to God's character.

The seventeen-year-old in chapter 3 accepted this limited concept. She loved Tom. She loved Tom more than God. God's will has been revealed for centuries. "Flee immorality ... Or do you not know that your body is a temple of the Holy Spirit who is in you, whom you have from God, and that you are not your own? For you have been bought with a price: therefore glorify God in your body" (1 Corinthians 6:18-20).

In contrast, Tom's will was, "Give me your body to gratify my lust." Only he didn't say it like that. He sugarcoated his true intention.

Tom: "Honey, we really love each other, don't we?"

She: "You know we do, Tom."

Tom: "Well, people who are in love don't have anything to hide or be ashamed of, do they?"

She: "I guess not."

Tom: "Well, what are we waiting for? All of our friends who really love each other sleep together. Do you love me that much?"

Well, apparently she did love him that much, but it was a love that was inconsistent with God's will and character. *Agape* love is patient (1 Corinthians 13:4). True love can wait until the wedding in spite of society's lower standards and in spite of strong desires. Jesus said, "If you love Me, you will keep My commandments" (John 14:15). Another time he said, "If you keep My commandments, you will abide in My love; just as I have kept My Father's commandments, and abide in His love" (John 15:10).

LOVE SACRIFICES

We express mature love by making necessary sacrifices. A man who says he loves his wife and children but spends little time with them should reevaluate the object of his love. The Christian who says he loves other people but always demands his rights should consider the example of Paul. "I know and am convinced in the Lord Jesus that nothing is unclean in itself; but to him who thinks anything to be unclean, to him it is unclean. For if because of food [meat offered to pagan idols] your brother is hurt, you are no longer walking according to love ... Therefore, if food causes my brother to stumble, I will never eat meat [offered to idols] again, that I might not cause my brother to stumble" (Romans 14:14, 15a; 1 Corinthians 8:13).

True love is willing to give up certain rights in order to help another person.

A gifted soloist will at times allow others to use their musical gifts. A gifted leader will allow his subordinates to be honored.

LOVE FORGIVES

When we love, we refuse to hold a grudge. Can you imagine the number of marriages that would be saved if people loved on this level? How many churches could be kept from splitting? "Love ... will hardly even notice when others do it wrong" (1 Corinthians 13:5d, TLB).

You've probably heard people say, "I'll never forget what he did to me!" Or "Don't accuse me of that. I can count at least

five different times when you did the very same thing to me."
What is their problem? Lack of forgiveness. When we refuse to
forgive, the offense goes into our mental file cabinet. We add to
that file until one day we're accused of something. Immediately
our computer begins operation. All the offenses committed by
our accuser surface from the subconscious. We can give the
name, rank, and serial number of every one of them. We've done
exactly what love doesn't do: keep an account of offenses.

Two biblical truths have helped me to love people at this level.
First, I think of how often I've sinned against God and how often
he has forgiven me. Then I hear Peter's question, "Lord, how
often shall my brother sin against me and I forgive him? Up to
seven times?" Jesus answered, "I do not say to you, up to seven
times, but up to seventy times seven" (Matthew 18:21, 22). In
other words, I must forgive another as often as God forgives me.

The second truth is contained in the parable of the king who
forgave a debtor of $10,000,000. But the debtor then refused to
forgive someone who owed him $2,000. The response of the
king when he heard the news is given in Matthew 18:31. "And
the king called before him the man he had forgiven and said,
'You evil-hearted wretch! Here I forgave you all that tremendous
debt, just because you asked me to—shouldn't you?'' (TLB). The
Scriptures are clear that I must not only forgive *as often* as God
forgives me, but I must also forgive *as much* as God forgives me.

Has anyone sinned against you more than you've sinned
against God? The Bible declares, "And be kind to one another,
tenderhearted, forgiving each other, *just as* God in Christ also has
forgiven you" (Ephesians 4:32).

LOVE ACCEPTS OTHERS

We love by being tolerant of others. The expression, "I can't
put up with him any longer," heard in the office, at school, at
church, and at home, is more of a commentary on the speaker
than on the one spoken about.

One of the marks of spiritual people is that they are "... showing forbearance to one another in love" (Ephesians 4:2). This

means that we put up with another's idiosyncrasies. We give him the privilege of expressing his views, even if they're contrary to our own. We often fail to express love in this way because we're so busy trying to manipulate others to conform to us. We play the role of God and attempt to create others, so to speak, in our own image.

Who is guilty? The wife who determines to remake her husband, just as she wants him. The teacher who wants his pupils to think exactly as he does. The parent who vicariously lives his child's life, hoping the child will fulfill his own unfulfilled ambitions. The leader who refuses to work with anyone who doesn't agree wholeheartedly with him. The teacher who can't stand the fickleness of the early teens. The perfectionist who despises the imperfections of others.

Each of these individuals needs to experience *agape* love and learn to put up with others. When I find this difficult, I try to think of what others have to put up with in me.

LOVE TELLS THE TRUTH

Have you thought of loving someone by telling him the truth? Sam is a gifted counselor. When his best friend, Bill, shared a problem with him, Sam sensed anger in his friend's heart. The problem became obvious, but Sam wrestled in his mind whether he should really propose the solution. He knew it would hurt Bill tremendously. Eventually Sam let love govern his gift of exhortation and pointed out Bill's anger to him. At first Bill denied it. Then he accused Sam of taking sides against him. Finally he agreed that it was true. He was mad at his boss. The next day Bill humbly walked into the office and apologized for his attitude. After his boss gained composure he said, "Bill, it takes a real man to do what you just did. I appreciate your honesty and strength of character. Maybe there's something about Christianity I've missed while I was growing up."

It's not easy to tell the complete truth when talking to a friend who is guilty of a bad attitude. It hurts you and it hurts him. But I've yet to hear of a surgeon who apologizes for hurting his patient.

He realizes that in order to remove gallstones he will have to cut. And the pain doesn't subside immediately after the operation. Within a few weeks, though, the patient feels better than he has for years.

Do you love enough to hurt when pain can't be avoided? The gifted counselor often faces this problem. The gifted preacher must commit himself to "Thus says the Lord in his Word."

Paul encouraged "speaking the truth in love" (Ephesians 4:15) and he practiced what he preached. He was forced by love for Peter and the rest of the Christians to rebuke Peter publicly. "But when Cephas came to Antioch, I opposed him to his face, because he stood condemned. For prior to the coming of certain men from James, he used to eat with the Gentiles; but when they came, he began to withdraw and hold himself aloof, fearing the party of the circumcision. And the rest of the Jews joined him in hypocrisy, with the result that even Barnabas was carried away by their hypocrisy" (Galatians 2:11-13). The truth was an embarrassment to everyone. Paul didn't enjoy opposing a personal friend in public. But because Peter's actions had led others astray, they had to be dealt with.

A word of caution. Before you launch out to speak the painful truth to someone, go over the following checklist.

(1) Is correction really needed?
(2) Am I the one to expose the problem?
(3) Am I confronting this person because I *love* him, or am I motivated by jealousy, bitterness, retaliation, or a self-exalting motive?
(4) Is my purpose to help that person or merely to expose his problem?
(5) Am I aware of my own weaknesses (Galatians 6:1)? Is my problem greater than his (Matthew 7:3-5), or identical to his (Romans 2:21-23)?

LOVE ACCEPTS THE TRUTH

If speaking the truth in love is difficult, try accepting the truth in love. How well do you accept criticism? Unless you're walking close to the Lord and have matured a great deal, you probably have difficulty in this area.

The problem is increased as our spiritual gifts become more fully developed. A ministerial student expects constructive criticism on his sermons, but a preacher of twenty years' experience will find criticism a hard pill to swallow. The young boy learning to work with his hands may admit he needs improvement, but a skilled craftsman may not tolerate negative comments on his latest masterpiece. "What in the world do you call that thing? It looks like a pile of junk!" A gifted teacher may want to expel a student who shoots holes in the teacher's logic before the rest of the class.

Can anything help us accept painful truth with love? Two principles provide a good beginning.

(1) Begin by asking the Lord to show you what areas in your life need improvement.

I am enjoying my ministry in our church at Fresno, but life was not always this pleasant. Some sticky problems during my first two years centered primarily around differences in philosophy of the local church and around several strong personalities.

When I first brought the problems to the Lord I asked him to change the people. But the people didn't change. I decided that God wasn't answering my prayers for a special reason. He wanted me to learn that until I changed my attitude toward the people, I couldn't expect them to change their attitude toward me.

After much frustration and soul-searching I began to say, "Lord, change this people's pastor." I agreed with the psalmist when he prayed, "Search *me*, O God, and know my heart; try *me* and know my anxious thoughts; and see if there be any hurtful way in *me*, and lead *me* in the everlasting way" (Psalm 139:23, 24).

God then began to answer. He showed me that I had an eye problem. You see, I had so focused on the splinters in the eyes of my people that I failed to see the logs in my own eyes (Matthew 7:3-5).

"They're childish and carnal," I used to think. "They don't

appreciate what I'm trying to do for them." Then I saw myself. "I am angry. *I* am childish, wanting them to conform to my ideas. I am unloving because they criticize." And though some of the criticism was based on misunderstanding, much of it was warranted. Eventually I was able to start thanking God for the criticism because I was able to see it as an answer to my prayers.

(2) Accept God's methods for changing you. God may use *circumstances* to uncover personal deficiencies. Have you ever had the feeling that you'd just about "arrived" in some area, and then found yourself in an impossible situation? Not knowing where to turn, you cried out to God. Then, in your hour of humility and weakness, you sensed his loving presence. You began to see life from a different perspective. And though you didn't enjoy the circumstances, they helped you draw closer to the Lord (Romans 8:28).

God also uses *his Word* to tell us what we need to change. Conviction may come through preaching at the worship service or during your personal devotions. It may come during a Sunday school class or a home Bible study. But whatever the circumstance, God's Word is able to pierce "as far as the division of soul and spirit, of both joints and marrow, and is able to judge the thoughts and intentions of the heart" (Hebrews 4:12).

God uses *people* to expose our lives with his light. And he doesn't reserve the task of criticism for our closest friends. He'll use the people at work (Christian and non-Christian), the kids at school, the people at church, family members. This means that God may be using your wife to point out areas that need changing in your life. He may use your children. He may choose a sarcastic, loud-mouthed hypocrite to point out your deficiencies.

The beautiful aspect of the whole process is to recognize that God is answering your prayers. If you ask him to search your heart, he will. If you ask him to show you what needs changing, he will. And then when he uses circumstances, his Word, or some individual as a tool to chisel away your square edges, you don't have to respond in anger. You don't have to point out the other person's fault. You don't have to justify your actions. You can respond quietly in your heart, "Thanks, Lord, I needed that."

LOVE DESTROYS BITTERNESS

Love is also expressed when you allow it to displace personal bitterness. Anger and bitterness have a way of destroying the embittered, along with their relationship to God. Prayer, Bible study, and Christian fellowship wither. Bitterness affects our emotional stability. Ever talk with a seemingly friendly person and innocently mention a certain name? The person's face suddenly turns red. His eyes enlarge. He speaks scathing words. You leave dismayed. Bitterness can turn an outwardly calm individual into a roaring lion. Bitterness can cause acute depression.

Bitterness can also affect the body. Anger and bitterness are a major cause of heart attacks. The blood pressure increases at a dangerous rate. The breathing becomes quick and short. The person becomes a prime candidate for a nervous breakdown or heart attack.

And bitterness does not stop with affecting only the embittered. It spreads like a cancer into human relationships. An employee becomes bitter toward his boss. He knows he has to get along with him in order to maintain his job, so he takes out his hostility on fellow workers. A teen-ager may come to school from a home that lacks the security and love for which he longs. He becomes bitter toward his parents, but releases his hostility on the school administration and teachers.

One of the most dangerous areas in which to harbor bitterness is the husband-wife relationship. A wife may become bitter toward her husband because he doesn't spend enough time with her. Or suppose she is growing in the Lord and he is spiritually dragging his feet. She may become bitter because he embarrasses her around church by his lack of interest.

On the other hand a husband may harbor hostility toward his wife for her management of the family finances. He wants to spend money on some gadget or project and she rejects the idea. He begins to feel like a little boy asking his mother for an ice cream cone before supper. His manhood is threatened and he determines somehow to get revenge.

Another husband may be married to a "never satisfied" type. His wife may be pushy: she wants him to make more money; she wants him to get that new position which just opened. She believes behind every successful man is an ambitious wife, so she constantly reminds him of all his friends who've made it big. She doesn't let him forget that anyone could do what he's doing. The husband's manhood is threatened. He may not show his resentment by threatening or shouting. He may just turn inward and determine to speak to her as little as possible. Or he may look in "greener pastures" for a woman who appreciates him.

There are hundreds of reasons why we become bitter toward one another, but there is no biblical allowance for bitterness. The Bible justifies "holy anger." Anger against inhumanity. Anger against ungodliness. But even such things don't produce bitterness and an unforgiving attitude in God.

What could be more inhumane or ungodly than falsely to accuse an innocent person of a crime and sentence him to death? Yet Jesus cried from the cross, "Father, forgive them." That's what love does. It forgives. It refuses to hold a grudge. It doesn't seek revenge, but rather reconciliation.

Paul's admonition to husbands can also be applied by wives, children, workers, and in any other human relationship. "Husbands, love your wives, and do not be embittered against them" (Colossians 3:19). In other words, if love is present in any relationship, bitterness is not. The best way to deal with bitterness is to replace it with love.

LOVE OVERCOMES FEAR

Another way to express *agape* is to allow it to overcome fear. The Apostle John wrote, "There is no fear in love; but perfect love casts out fear, because fear involves punishment, and the one who fears is not perfected in love" (1 John 4:18).

What produces fear in your heart? Possible job loss? Financial failure? Loss of health? Loss of a loved one? Your eternal destiny? Fear that you're losing your mind? Fear is as universal to human life as the common cold. And all fear isn't bad.

We should fear to drink anything labeled "poison." We should fear allowing our children to run across a busy street. We should be afraid to let a small child play by an unattended swimming pool. We should fear the consequences of not paying the IRS its due. We should fear when we travel at 70 mph when the speed limit is 55.

Other fears are unhealthy and unnecessary. There is no reason to fear not having what we need. God promises, "But seek first His kingdom and His righteousness; and all these things [food and clothing] shall be added to you" (Matthew 6:33). It is pointless to fear eternal separation from God. God promises that "the one who comes to Me I will certainly not cast out" (John 6:37). It is futile to fear that "no one loves me." The Bible guarantees, "For I am convinced that neither death, nor life, nor angels, nor principalities, nor things present, nor things to come, nor powers, nor height, nor depth, nor any other created thing, shall be able to separate us from the love of God, which is in Christ Jesus our Lord" (Romans 8:38, 39). To fear adverse circumstances is useless. The Bible assures us that "God causes all things to work together for good to those who love God, to those who are called according to His purpose" (Romans 8:28).

What does John mean when he writes that perfect love removes fear? John is talking about believing God's promises. "By this, love is perfected with us, that we may have confidence in the day of judgment" (1 John 4:17). How can we have confidence and not fear at such a time? By believing God's promises. "Believe in the Lord Jesus, and you shall be saved" (Acts 16:31). "But as many as received Him, to them He gave the right to become children of God, even to those who believe in His name" (John 1:12).

If you have acted upon these truths by inviting Christ into your life, you need not fear eternity. In fact you can now anticipate a wonderful eternal future with Christ. Further, if you love God to the point of believing he controls all circumstances, there is no need to fear problems, failures, or any other adversity.

Love also affects our relating to strangers. We often fear that the stranger is better looking, wealthier, or more successful, so we tend to greet him cautiously. But if we loved the stranger and loved God, there would be no need to fear. Love for God provides our personal security. Love for the stranger provides an opportunity to discover his needs, to share ourselves, and to share God's love for him. Mature love will remove this type of unnecessary fear.

LOVE DISCIPLINES

A serious misapplication of love arises in the realm of discipline. Love can be shown by discipline. Too many parents argue, "I can't spank my child. I love him too much. How can you hurt someone you deeply love?"

Years ago I met a young boy who was extremely rebellious. He rebelled against his parents' authority. He rebelled against authority at school and eventually quit. He rebelled against the authority of church leadership and stopped attending church regularly. To my knowledge he still lives in inner rebelliousness against the authority of God over his life. And though he will have to answer to God for his own actions, I believe he placed his finger on the beginning of the problem during a conversation. He sadly said, "I really question whether my dad loves me." I asked him to explain. He continued, "Ever since I was a little boy I never remember him spanking me. How can a father love his son and let him get away with anything he wants to do?" When I spoke to the father he said, "I just can't spank my children."

What a contrast to the love of our heavenly Father. "For those whom the Lord loves He disciplines" (Hebrews 12:6a). "He disciplines us for our good, that we may share His holiness" (Hebrews 12:10b).

Love, demonstrated through discipline, has the loved one's best interest in mind. If a small child reaches out to a hot iron, he will be stopped by a loving parent. The child may cry because he doesn't understand the danger. It may hurt the child's feelings that he isn't allowed to touch the iron, but the parent knows that it will hurt him more if he does touch.

Discipline is like that. It may provide a small hurt to prevent a greater pain. "All discipline for the moment seems not to be joyful, but sorrowful; yet to those who have been trained by it, afterwards it yields the peaceful fruit of righteousness" (Hebrews

12:11). To prevent the agony and frustration of a spiritually unfruitful life, discipline must be administered at times.

The home is not the only realm in which discipline is often withheld. Today we experience little discipline in the church. The man with money is treated with partiality. He doesn't have to toe the line the way others do. The soloist in the choir is allowed to go on a rampage now and then because her gift is so needed. A "pillar" is permitted to bully and whip people into shape because he is from an important local family. Turning our backs on the failures of character of those who are highly gifted, we may fail to discipline them when they are out of order.

During the first century, discipline was part of church life. Paul disciplined Peter (Galatians 2:11-15). God disciplined Ananias and Sapphira through Peter (Acts 5:1-11). The Corinthians were rebuked for refusing to discipline one of their members (1 Corinthians 5).

Discipline may take the form of a stern rebuke (Galatians 2:11-15), or of excommunication (1 Corinthians 5:2). A local church may remove an individual from a specific responsibility, or even from fellowship. Unloving? Dogmatic? No. If a church loves its members enough to protect them from questionable behavior, it must discipline. If the church sees one of its members setting a poor example, especially while holding a position of influence, then love will best be demonstrated by discipline.

LOVE HONORS OTHERS

Another means of showing love is by honoring others. Paul writes, "Be devoted to one another in brotherly love; give preference to one another in honor" (Romans 12:10). The same exhortation is given in other passages. "Do nothing from selfishness or empty conceit, but with humility of mind let each of you regard one another as more important than himself; do not merely look out for your own personal interests, but also for the interests of others" (Philippians 2:3, 4).

The Apostle Peter lifts this act of love out of the limited realm of loving only other Christians. He writes, "Honor all men; love the brotherhood, fear God, honor the king" (1 Peter 2:17). How can you and I love others by honoring them?

(1) To honor others is to respect them, their interests, their feelings. Walk in their shoes and see life from their perspective. Respect them as individuals with needs, desires, and viewpoints that may be contrary to your own. You need not agree with everything they do or say, but you respect them for their position. You respect them for their humanness, created in the image of God. You respect them because God loves them. You respect them because Christ died for them.

(2) To honor others is to express appreciation to them. Someone does a favor for us. If we're thankful, we should express our appreciation in words or by some thoughtful act in return.

What is God's view on showing appreciation? Jesus healed ten lepers one day, but only one returned to express appreciation. Jesus asked, "Were there not ten cleansed? But the nine—where are they? Were none found who turned back to give glory to God, except this foreigner?" (Luke 17:17, 18).

A friend of mine has the reputation of "going out of his way" for others. If a man needs a job, he helps him find one. If a stranger needs gas, my friend fills the tank free of charge. But in the majority of cases, he never hears from them again.

The Apostle Paul continually expressed his appreciation for the life and ministry of believers (Romans 1:8; 1 Corinthians 1:4-7; Ephesians 1:15, 16; Philippians 1:3). He thanked the Christians at Philippi for their financial support (Philippians 4:14-19). He expressed appreciation to Prisca and Aquila who risked their lives for him (Romans 16:3, 4). He thanked Mary for her hard work (Romans 16:6). Andronicus and Junias were honored because they were outstanding apostles (Romans 16:7).

Paul gave credit where it was due. He wasn't playing politics. He wasn't flattering others, hoping to get ahead in life. Rather, he showed his love by honoring others.

(3) To honor others is to befriend them, especially those not yet accepted by "the group." As you read the letters of Paul you get the impression that he was always quite popular. But that isn't the case.

Paul found it difficult to break into Christian society. He had a fearful reputation among the early believers. He had been the "Gestapo" to the disciples, "breathing threats and murder" against them (Acts 9:1). Therefore, when Saul of Tarsus came into a personal relationship with Jesus Christ and wanted to be accepted by the disciples, he experienced a cold reception. No one trusted him. They thought it was a trick.

One disciple, however, didn't share the suspicion of the others. His name was Barnabas ("son of encouragement"). Luke, the historian, recorded the scene. "But Barnabas took hold of him and brought him to the apostles and described to them how he had seen the Lord on the road, and that He had talked to him, and how at Damascus he had spoken out boldly in the name of Jesus" (Acts 9:27, 28). Upon further testimony from Barnabas, the disciples accepted Paul into their fellowship. The result: "So the church throughout all Judea and Galilee and Samaria enjoyed peace, being built up; and, going on in the fear of the Lord and in the comfort of the Holy Spirit, it continued to increase" (Acts 9:31).

We have discovered in our own church that the number one reasons why visitors return a second time is that someone befriends them. A visitor is not honored by being ignored. He is honored when he is treated like any other member.

SUMMARY

Learning how to love is like discovering new stars in the heavens. You see some with the naked eye, but if you use a telescope you see many more that the eye alone cannot discern. Likewise, as you love people in one way you soon discover ten more ways to express love.

This chapter describes only a small sample of how you can love. Yet as you compare these ideas with your own life you'll admit, "I haven't yet experienced perfect love."

This is where the Holy Spirit makes so much difference. To consistently love like this is a human impossibility. But the fruit of the Spirit is love. *Agape* love. *Giving* love. I've personally discovered that the only way I can possibly love some people is to place the problem in God's hands.

My first step is to confess my own inability to love as I know I should:

"Father, I confess to you that I don't love Tom Smith. He is obnoxious. His personality really turns me off. But I know you love him. I want to love him, but haven't been able to."

Then I ask the Lord to deal with my real feelings:

"Lord, whenever I'm around him I get uptight. I feel resentment and hostility. Replace these feelings with warmth and concern. Help me to see Tom's real needs. Help me understand why he does what he does."

Finally, I ask God to provide an opportunity to show genuine love:

"Lord, I also pray that you'll open opportunities for me to show acts of love toward Tom. Show me how to meet his needs. Thank you, God, that your Holy Spirit will begin to love Tom through me. Amen."

When God does open that opportunity, your first feelings may be resentful. But thank God that you don't have to depend on your feelings. He has given you that opportunity to *show love,* even though you may not yet *feel* love. As you show love by a kind word or thoughtful act, the feeling of love will eventually follow.

No longer are you bound to manufacture love in your own strength. You can begin to put aside the false smile, thinking in your heart, "I can't stand that person." God will take the frustration and hypocrisy out of trying to love the unlovely.

Love is one of the qualities of God's character that must govern our spiritual gifts. The gift of tongues without love is just a loud noise. The gifts of prophecy, knowledge, and faith without love are nothing. The gift of giving without love is unprofitable (1 Corinthians 13:1-3). But when love is integrated with spiritual gifts, we have an ample supply of spiritual power.

when all else fails, rejoice!

The phone rang late at night. I was studying for an exam the next day. My friend said, "Rick, you have a long distance call." I never liked long distance calls late at night, especially when I was away from home. As I answered, I heard dad's forcedly composed voice on the other end. "Rick, Mother just went home to be with the Lord." In the few seconds of silence that followed I was filled with shock, unbelief, grief, and the reality of God's presence. I said the first thing that came to my mind: "Dad, 'the Lord gave and the Lord has taken away. Blessed be the name of the Lord.' I'll be home as soon as I can."

I maintained composure until I got back to my dorm room. My roommate's questioning eyes followed me over to my bed. "Was it bad news, Rick?"

All I could say was, "Mother's dead!"

As I lay on my bed sobbing, several of my friends came into the room to pack my bags. It would be about a two-hour trip from Philadelphia to Lancaster that time of night. By the time I'd gotten over the first emotional trauma, my friends and I began to pray. After we prayed, I began to sing "How Great Thou Art."

One of my classmates loaned me his car. I was on my way home. The typical questions were running through my mind. "Why Mother, Lord? She was only forty-two. Why so sudden? Why now, when I'm just a sophomore in college? Dad's going to be so alone."

I was quoting as many Scriptures as I could, to keep my mind occupied with God. I was singing. Then I was crying, quoting, singing, and crying again and again.

As I approached the outskirts of Philadelphia I saw three university students hitchhiking. I pulled over and asked where they were headed. "Villanova."

"Fine, I'm going right past the school," I replied. The fellows asked where I was going at one A.M. I shared my destination and purpose.

"But how can you be so happy about everything?"

I replied, "Right now I'm just about cried out. I'm rejoicing because I know where Mother is. When she was a girl she invited Jesus Christ into her life. He has forgiven her sins, so I have no doubts that she is with Jesus. And some day I'm going to be with her. That's why I'm rejoicing. I'm learning that you can rejoice in spite of a broken heart."

Needless to say there was no theological debate with these students. The Lord provided a beautiful opportunity to demonstrate that faith in a loving, caring God makes a tremendous difference in how we face adversity.

I've seen joy on the face of a young woman whose husband had walked out on her and her children. Brokenhearted, humiliated, and filled with overwhelming sorrow, she could still rejoice *in the Lord.*

A young couple learned that their daughter was retarded. After years of frustration and self-pity, one day the mother heard God ask, "Joyce, what do you have to be thankful about?"

Joyce thought for a while and then said, "Thank you, Lord, for the flowers and the trees. Thank you for a loving and understanding husband. Thank you for my health. Thank you..." That was the turning point in her life. Today the Lord has blessed her abundantly as she ministers to other women with all kinds of problems. They can never say, "Joyce, you just don't understand. You've never felt lonely, frustrated, and helpless."

Paul told the Philippian believers, "Rejoice in the Lord always; again I will say, rejoice!" (Philippians 4:4). Do you know when Paul made that statement? He was sitting in a stuffy, filthy prison cell. He was chained to guards continuously. He experienced sorrow. He needed encouragement. He would rather die and be with the Lord than face another day in that prison (Philippians 1, 2).

But in spite of his circumstances and feelings he wrote an epistle of joy. He prayed with joy. He rejoiced that the gospel was being proclaimed even though he was locked up. He rejoiced at the privilege of dying for his faith if it would come to that. He encouraged his readers to rejoice (Philippians 3:1; 4:4). He rejoiced that he wasn't forgotten by them (Philippians 4:10).

JOY IS NOT EVERYONE'S EXPERIENCE

misplaced faith

Sorrow, pain, loneliness, frustration and *joy*? How is it possible? And why doesn't everyone experience joy when things go wrong?

The first common barrier to a life of joy is misplaced faith, relying on the wrong things or people. Everybody has faith. (Even the atheist has faith. When he boards a plane, he believes that the engineers knew what they were doing when they designed the plane. He expects that the craftsmen who put the plane together had their heads screwed on right. He believes that the pilot and crew know how to maneuver the aircraft safely. He trusts the control tower to get him safely from one destination to another.) But we often misplace our faith, relying on something other than the one true God, made known through his Son Jesus.

We place our reliance on *money*. Millions of Americans have been struck low by a rapidly declining stock market. Some are losing retirement money, others their life savings. Some lose what they have never personally possessed, only borrowed. Now they owe Peter and Paul. They can no longer take from Peter to pay Paul. Inflation and depression are wiping them out.

Those whose faith is transferred from God to money have nothing to rejoice about; the haunting words of the Apostle Paul have been fulfilled so accurately. "But those who want to get rich fall into temptation and a snare and many foolish and harmful desires which plunge men into ruin and destruction. For the love of money is a root of all sorts of evil, and some by longing for it have wandered away from the faith, and pierced themselves with many a pang... Instruct those who are rich in this present world *not to be conceited or to fix their hope on the uncertainty of riches, but on God,* who richly supplies us with all things to enjoy'' (1 Timothy 6:9, 10, 17).

Money is so elusive, so uncertain, especially in a fluctuating or declining economy. But even in a stable economy, you cannot trust money. Jesus said, "Do not lay up for yourselves treasures upon earth, where moth and rust destroy, and where thieves break in and steal. But lay up for yourselves treasures in heaven, where neither moth nor rust destroys, and where thieves do not break in or steal" (Matthew 6:19, 20).

Remember that beautiful wool sweater? Today it has moth holes. What about the brand-new car you bought just a few years ago? Today it shows signs of rust, nicks, scratches, and dents. Then there's that precious heirloom that was stolen. The gold ring. The new stereo. The color TV. If thieves haven't diminished your possessions, there are fire, hurricane, accident, earthquake, tornado, hail, and flood.

Another hindrance to joy is a misplaced focus on the value of a *healthy body.* I believe in physical fitness. My body is the temple of the Holy Spirit (1 Corinthians 6:19). I don't believe that God is glorified by an overweight, overworked, fatigued body. Sermons against the abuses of the body name smoking, drinking, and drugs as the big three. But excess weight is excused as a minor problem. Overwork is honored as diligence. Too little sleep is correlated with great sacrifice.

In contrast, God condemned gluttony (Proverbs 23:21). He made provision against overwork by establishing the Sabbath. He warned against lack of sleep. "It is senseless for you to work so hard from early morning until late at night, fearing you will starve to death; for God wants his loved ones to get their proper rest" (Psalm 127:2, TLB). Physical fitness is essential if we're going to "glorify God" in our bodies (1 Corinthians 6:20).

There is a vast difference, however, between keeping the body in good condition and trusting in the body for our source of joy. The body may become the god of the beauty queen or athlete.

Then when health breaks, or the body grows old or becomes disfigured, an immense vacuum is created. Having used their bodies to "get their man," some women discover later that their man is now looking at a new model. The professional athlete stakes his livelihood on a healthy body. But if age or accident claim his health, he's in trouble.

Satan knows how much we value our health. When he wanted to tempt Job to curse God, Satan said, "A man will give anything to save his life. Touch his body with sickness and he will curse you to your face" (Job 2:4, 5, TLB).

Certainly, you and I want good health. I praise God for my health. But I rejoice in God in spite of the pain in my side due to badly bruised or broken ribs. I visit hospitals hoping to comfort those who have gone through major surgery or those who have been told they have terminal cancer. Yet as I begin to minister to these men and women, they often encourage and challenge me. How sad that in those same hospitals lie embittered and angry patients who curse God and live out their days in self-pity. The latter have trusted in their health for happiness and joy. The former have placed their faith in God.

A third object of misplaced faith can be the *family*. To many people, their family is their life. When separation, divorce, or death takes a family member, their world collapses.

That Old Testament saint, Job, lost his wealth, his health, and his family in a short time. "Then his wife said to him, 'Curse God and die!' But he said to her, 'You speak as one of the foolish women speaks. Shall we indeed accept good from God and not accept adversity?' In all this Job did not sin with his lips" (Job 2:8-10). Misplaced faith in wealth, health, or family will not allow joy when they are removed from us.

Another addition to this list is *achievement*. Everybody enjoys being a winner. We want our favorite team to win. We desire our children to do well in school. We want success for ourselves. But joy in achievement is temporal. Remember when you won that school championship? At the time it was so important, but today you barely remember it. Those trophies and ribbons packed away in a box out in the garage were your whole life at one time, but today they're saved for children, grandchildren, and old teammates. The position for which you were at one time willing to do anything is now a routine and frustrating job. The picture in the local newspaper has faded with the memories. The salary you strived for and achieved is no longer sufficient to meet your family's needs. All your successes have become so unimportant.

Few people had the success of Solomon, the third king of Israel. How did he evaluate his success? "I, the Preacher, was king of Israel, living in Jerusalem. And I applied myself to search for understanding about everything in the universe. I discovered that the lot of man, which God has dealt to him, is not a happy one. It is all foolishness, chasing the wind. What is wrong cannot be righted; it is water over the dam; and there is no use thinking of what might have been. I said to myself, 'Look, I am better educated than any of the kings before me in Jerusalem. I have greater wisdom and knowledge' ... Then I tried to find fulfillment by inaugurating a great public works program: homes, vineyards, gardens, parks and orchards for myself, and reservoirs to hold the water to irrigate my plantations ... I also bred great herds and flocks, more than any of the kings before me. I collected silver and gold as taxes from many kings and provinces. In the cultural arts, I organized men's and women's choirs and orchestras ... So I became greater than any of the kings in Jerusalem before me ... So I turned in despair from hard work as the answer to my search for satisfaction ... So what does a man get for all his hard work? Days full of sorrow and grief, and restless, bitter nights. It is all utterly ridiculous" (Selections from Ecclesiastes 1, 2, TLB).

Another area of misplaced faith may be an inordinate dependence upon *people*. I'm not implying that we should distrust everyone. At the same time, our trust cannot be in people alone. If it is, we will be greatly disappointed. Even our friends can fail us greatly. Jesus Christ had twelve close friends. One denied him, another betrayed him, and the other ten abandoned him. The Apostle Paul was forsaken by his friend Demas (2 Timothy 4:10). The psalmist even recognized the possibility of parents' forsaking their children (Psalm 27:10).

Faith and confidence in God produce joy. But when we place our faith in material things, health, family, success, or people, we fail to experience the joy that God wants to give.

lack of faith in God's ability

A second reason why so few of us experience joy in adversity is that we lack faith in God's ability to provide for our needs.

The Bible says, "God loves a cheerful giver" (2 Corinthians 9:7). God has blessed you financially. Over the years you've given to many Christian works, including your local church. You admit you've not always given cheerfully, and lately it's become a drag. Some of the people in the church keep expecting you to bail them out of every financial difficulty they get the church into. With the economy as uncertain as it is, you're wondering about cutting back on your giving. Maybe it would be better to put a little more away for a rainy day. Depression may be just around the corner. Although the Bible says, "My God shall supply all your needs" (Philippians 4:19), you conclude it's better to save than be sorry.

We rob ourselves of God's joy because we fail to believe him. In spite of his promises to provide for us, we question stepping out in faith—and in the process we play God. We take his responsibility upon ourselves. If you feel under pressure, it may be that you, a finite (limited) being, are attempting to accomplish an infinite (unlimited) task.

God is responsible for physical needs

Even spiritually gifted individuals may lose the joy of utilizing their gift because of over-concern for material needs. A missionary who is going to a foreign land to begin a new work is a kind of modern-day apostle. He faces new experiences as he begins his deputation. Will he have enough money to go to the field? Will his friends continue their support once he's out there, thousands of miles away?

The pastor and traveling evangelist may be asking similar questions. Salaries and love offerings may be slim, yet bills continue to mount. Where will the physical supplies come from?

God's promise to his children comes from the lips of Jesus. "Don't worry about things—food, drink, and clothes. For you already have life and a body—and they are far more important than what to eat or wear. Look at the birds! They don't worry about what to eat—they don't need to sow or reap or store up food—for your heavenly Father feeds them. And *you are far more valuable to him* than they are ... And if God cares so wonderfully for flowers that are here today and gone tomorrow, won't he more surely care for you, O men of little faith?" (Matthew 6:25, 26, 30, TLB).

God is responsible for safety needs

Another basic need is our safety or security. We have insurance, investments, and trust funds for economic security. As we grow older our concern focuses on our health. Some teachers worry about their safety as they teach in the ghettos. And how safe is a person who uses his gift of showing mercy by working in an institution with the mentally ill? Can we trust God for safety and security?

God has promised to ensure our *physical safety*. The psalmist declared, "We live within the shadow of the Almighty, sheltered by the God who is above all gods. This I declare, that he alone is my refuge, my place of safety; he is my God, and I am trusting him. For he rescues you from every trap, and protects you from the fatal plague. He will shield you with his wings. They will shelter you. His faithful promises are your armor. Now you don't need to be afraid of the dark any more, nor fear the dangers of the day; nor dread the plagues of darkness, nor disasters in the morning" (Psalm 91:1-6, TLB).

Insurance, investments, locks on doors, and other safety precautions are valid. These are ways in which God protects us. But when we face physical danger head-on, there is only one to whom we can turn.

The Lord also promises to supply *economic security*. Paul wrote, "And it is he who will supply all your needs from his riches in glory, because of what Christ Jesus has done for us" (Philippians 4:19, TLB). It's important to understand that Paul was writing to a group of Christians who had just sent him a financial gift. They had given sacrificially to meet his needs. The apostle assured them that God is no man's debtor. God does not promise to provide economic security for the stingy tightwad. He gives to the generous giver. "But remember this—if you give little you will get little. A farmer who plants just a few seeds will get only a small crop, but if he plants much, he will reap much. Everyone must make up his own mind as to how much he should give. Don't force anyone to give more than he really wants to, for cheerful givers are the ones God prizes. God is able to make it up to you by giving you everything you need and more, so that there will not only be enough for your own needs, but plenty left over to give joyfully to others. It is as the Scriptures say: 'The godly man gives generously to the poor. His good deeds will be an honor to him forever.' For God, who gives seed to the farmer to plant, and later on, good crops to harvest and eat, will give you more and more seed to plant and will make it grow so *that you can give away more and more* fruit from your harvest" (2 Corinthians 9:6-10, TLB).

God's provision extends to our *emotional stability*. The prophet Isaiah promised, "He will keep in perfect peace all those who trust in him, whose thoughts turn often to the Lord" (Isaiah 26:3, TLB).

God also promises to provide for our *spiritual security*. Jesus vowed, "My sheep recognize my voice, and I know them, and they follow me. I give them eternal life and they shall never perish. No one shall snatch them away from me, for my Father has given them to me, and he is more powerful than anyone else, so no one can kidnap them from me. I and my Father are one" (John 10:27-30, TLB).

A large bank account, promises of a future inheritance, a good job, a dream house in an affluent suburb, a good education, or any other common security is no guarantee that we will be safe and serene. Our only security is in the one who promises to provide for our physical, economic, emotional, and spiritual safety.

God is responsible for "belonging needs"

Most people have a need to "belong," to be loved, to have friends, to be recognized by others. Haven't you often asked,

"Do people really like me?" or "Will I be accepted?"

Dr. Howard Hendricks speaks of the kid who arrives on campus with his umbilical cord in his hand, looking for a place to plug in. The child needs to belong to his parents. The teen wants to belong to his gang, his team, the cheerleaders, the band. The college student goes for the fraternity, sorority, or the Christian group on campus. The adult searches for acceptance in various clubs, civic organizations, or church.

I can remember how I craved to belong to some small group when I was in high school. Though I was in the band and on the gymnastics team, I looked for a social group. My high school was on the other side of town, so I didn't have a natural geographical social grouping. My in-group was scattered around town.

Finally in my senior year, one of the fellows bought a jeep. One night after a football game several of my friends were driving home in Ed's jeep. They asked if I wanted to go along. Without hesitation I jumped into the jeep and off we went. That was the beginning of our "Jeepsters." Instead of dating girls every Friday or Saturday, we'd tear around town in the jeep, never getting into trouble, but having a fantastic time. As our fame grew that year for some of the escapades we got into, my "belonging" needs were satisfied.

God meets the belonging need in our hearts through the Body of Christ. "And all those who had believed were together, and had all things in common ... And day by day continuing with one mind in the temple, and breaking bread from house to house, they were taking their meals together with gladness and sincerity of heart, praising God, and having favor with all the people. And the Lord was adding to their number day by day those who were being saved" (Acts 2:44, 46, 47).

Before Pentecost there were many kinds of "belonging" groups. Jews remained with Jews and Gentiles stayed with Gentiles. Slaves had nothing in common with their masters. Women were not even second-class citizens. But observe what happens when the Holy Spirit places a person into the Body of Christ. "For all of you who were baptized into Christ have clothed yourselves with Christ. There is neither Jew nor Greek, there is neither slave nor free man, there is neither male nor female; for you are all one in Christ Jesus" (Galatians 3:27, 28).

The Body doesn't accept only certain persons into its ranks, such as apostles, prophets, evangelists, and pastor-teachers. Whatever your gift, public or private, great or small, you belong to the Body. "God has placed the members, each one of them, in the body, just as He desired ... And the eye cannot say to the hand, 'I have no need of you'; or again the head to the feet, 'I have no need of you' " (1 Corinthians 12:18, 21).

In the Body there should be no discrimination. If an individual possesses Christ as Savior he is part of the Body and his belonging need should be met by that Body. Sometimes, however, a local church may exclude some of those whom God has accepted. If you're shut out, your need is still fulfilled by God's promise. "All that the Father gives Me shall come to Me; and the one who comes to Me I will certainly not cast out" (John 6:37). The psalmist recognized to whom he belonged when he wrote, "For my father and mother have forsaken me, but the Lord will take me up" (Psalm 27:10).

Your joy will disappear if you depend solely on human groupings to meet your belonging needs. Parents may fail you, friends may forsake you, even the church may ignore you. But you belong to God if Christ is in your life. You are a gifted person (Romans 12:6). You are part of the universal Body of Christ (1 Corinthians 12:13). You belong (1 Corinthians 3:23). You are loved (Romans 8:37-39). You are accepted (Romans 15:7). Therefore, "Rejoice in the Lord always. Again I say rejoice!" (Philippians 4:4).

But what about the need for approval? It's one thing to know that you belong, that you are accepted. But how will your "esteem" needs be fulfilled by God?

God is responsible for "esteem needs"

"Esteem needs" include our need for self-respect and for respect from others—that is, our desire for self-worth, self-confidence, and status. Will I make the team? Am I smart enough? Am I pretty? Will I get that position? What more should I do to prove myself?

Over the years a lot of us turn into people-pleasers. Some choose vocations simply to please their parents. Others major in a specific field to please a respected teacher. Pleasing others isn't necessarily bad. Paul tells us we should please another when it is for that one's good. "Now we who are strong ought to bear the weaknesses of those without strength and not just please ourselves. Let each of us please his neighbor for his good, to his edification. For even Christ did not please Himself; but as it is written, 'The reproaches of those who reproached Thee fell upon Me' " (Romans 15:1-3).

The Apostle warns, however, that pleasing others for the purpose of selfish advance is wrong. "For our exhortation does not come from error or impurity or by way of deceit; but just as we have been approved by God to be entrusted with the gospel, so we speak, *not as pleasing men* but God, who examines our hearts. For we never came with flattering speech, as you know, nor with a pretext for greed—God is witness—nor did we seek glory from men, either from you or from others" (1 Thessalonians 2:3-6).

Paul's word to slaves (workers) emphasizes the same truth. "Slaves, in all things obey those who are your masters on earth, *not with external service, as those who merely please men,* but with sincerity of heart, fearing the Lord. Whatever you do, do your work heartily, as for the Lord rather than for men" (Colossians 3:22, 23).

I realize that these exhortations are completely alienated from the way the average person (including some who are Christians) operates: "If I don't push ahead and prove myself, I'll never make it to the top. I want to count. I want people to know I exist." God realizes your need to do what is important. He knows you want to count, but he has a better way. God's formula simply stated is this: "The fastest way up is down. Exaltation comes through humiliation." Jesus put it another way. "The first shall be last and the last shall be first," or "whoever wishes to become great among you shall be your servant" (Mark 10:43).

OK, I'll stop quoting formulas. But remember God's Word through Isaiah. " 'For My thoughts are not your thoughts, neither are your ways My ways,' declares the Lord. 'For as the heavens are higher than the earth, so are My ways higher than your ways, and My thoughts than your thoughts' " (Isaiah 55:8, 9). God's approach to meeting your esteem needs is foreign to our cultural conditioning.

There is little joy in the life of one who continues to shove ahead. When the end justifies the means, there will be little to rejoice over. The tragedy of Watergate should embed this truth into our lives.

Both James and Peter describe the means to meet esteem needs. "Humble yourselves in the presence of the Lord, and He will exalt you" (James 4:10). "Humble yourselves, therefore, under the mighty hand of God, that He may exalt you at the proper time" (1 Peter 5:6). Does that really work? Can I trust God to exalt me if I humble myself? If I turn my future over to him and say, "Lord, I want whatever you want. I depend on you to meet my need for esteem," will he answer my prayer?

Look at the life of his Son. Jesus was exalted after he humbled himself. "And being found in appearance as a man, *He humbled Himself* by becoming obedient to the point of death, even death on a cross. Therefore also *God highly exalted Him,* and bestowed on Him the name which is above every name" (Philippians 2:8, 9).

Consider Saul of Tarsus. Before he humbled himself, he was a self-seeking, self-exalting, fanatical Pharisee. He was making a name for himself as he persecuted the church. But as he was on his way to Damascus he met the Lord (Acts 9). The Lord humbled this young zealot through suffering, "For I will show him how much he must suffer for My name's sake" (Acts 9:16; cf. 2 Corinthians 11:23-28). As God humbled Saul he could honestly declare, "Most gladly, therefore, I will rather boast about my weaknesses, that the power of Christ may dwell in me" (2 Corinthians 12:9). That young Pharisee may never have reached his early goals in life, but as he was humbled by God, and as he rejoiced in his humiliation, the Lord exalted him in the eyes of the world. His gifts brought him before great men (Proverbs 18:16). His humiliation (Philippians 3:7) resulted in his exaltation (Acts 9:15).

Freedom comes as we relax in God's program and timing.

Believe that he has gifted you and wants to use that gift. He will open doors. He will give you a sense of worth. He will give you self-confidence and self-respect. He will cause others to respect you. He has taken full responsibility to meet your esteem needs, but you must willingly humble yourself before him and work in his timetable.

God is responsible for self-fulfillment needs

Ever ask yourself, "Is there something else I could be doing with my life?" Many people are totally bored with their jobs. When men, in particular, reach their forties and fifties they begin to dream about the great things they might have done if.... Some change from one job to another. Others resort to hobbies for fulfillment. Others seek creativity after they become financially secure; they retire early and do what they've always wanted to do.

Once you turn this area of need over to God you won't have to live in frustration. If you're willing to abandon security, prestige, reputation, and any other hindrance between you and creative fulfillment, you can experience God's promises. Can you imagine the fulfillment Jesus experienced when he told his Father, "I brought glory to you here on earth by doing everything you told me to" (John 17:4, TLB). At the end of Paul's life he could say, "I have fought the good fight, I have finished the course, I have kept the faith" (2 Timothy 4:7).

The person who abandons his future to God and allows the Lord to fulfill his life will experience satisfaction. On one occasion Peter reminded Jesus that he and the disciples had willingly sacrificed for him. "Then Peter said to him, 'We left everything to follow you. What will we get out of it?' And Jesus replied, 'When I, the Messiah, shall sit upon my glorious throne in the Kingdom, you my disciples shall certainly sit on twelve thrones judging the twelve tribes of Israel. And *anyone* who gives up his home, brothers, sisters, father, mother, wife, children, or property, to follow me, shall receive a hundred times as much in return, and shall have eternal life' " (Matthew 19:27-29, TLB).

God may want some to leave their home and family ties to go

to other places and serve him. Some will leave their economic security, as several couples did in the Windsor Park Evangelical Free Church in Winnipeg, Manitoba. Don Wicks, a former member of that church, wrote about the Canadian revival of the early 1970s: "For Bill and Kathy Toews, revival meant leaving the real estate business to work full-time for Child Evangelism Fellowship. For Morely Lee, a professor at the University of Manitoba, it meant quitting that position in favor of a full-time camp ministry in Ontario. Revival largely influenced John and Myrtle Doerksen to forsake a business career in Canada in favor of foreign missionary service. Mr. Doerksen now uses his accounting skills in the office of an international mission in Ethiopia" ("The Revival Has Not Ended," *The Evangelical Beacon*, Sept. 17, 1974, p. 11).

Recently in our Fresno congregation a young man resigned from the faculty of Fresno State University. He and his wife were new Christians. They had fulfilled the so-called "American dream"—good job, two cars, color TV, economic security—but they couldn't find lasting satisfaction. So they said, "All right, Lord, what plan do you have for us? What should we do? Where should we go?" Within a few months several opportunities for Christian service opened. Today Doug serves the Lord in the drama department at a Christian college, and they are rejoicing in God's way for them.

But the Lord cannot be put into a box. He does not call everyone to leave a job. He tells others to stay where they are and find fulfillment by the way they work, by recognizing that in whatever they're doing they can glorify him and minister to the needs of others.

personal sin

Another major barrier to joy is personal sin. The Bible describes David as a man after God's own heart (Acts 13:22). His psalms are full of rejoicing. He experienced joy when he meditated upon God. He experienced joy even when his enemies pursued him (Psalm 35:1-9).

But in a time of weakness he took another man's wife. To

cover his tracks he sent her husband to the front lines, and the husband was killed. In spite of the fact that the world promises joy from an extramarital affair, David, like thousands of others, found guilt and misery.

Finally he confessed his sin to God. "Against Thee, Thee only, I have sinned, and done what is evil in Thy sight" (Psalm 51:4a). Then he asked the Lord, "Restore to me the *joy* of Thy salvation" (Psalm 51:12a). In another psalm he wrote, "When I kept silent about my sin, my body wasted away through my groaning all day long. For day and night Thy hand was heavy upon me; my vitality was drained away as with the fever-heat of summer" (Psalm 32:3, 4).

Sin has a way of limiting joy. The gifted teacher will not experience joy when using his gift if he refuses to acknowledge sin. The gifted musician may play or sing beautifully. His music may even become a temporal escape from sin's guilt. But the joy that flows from the Holy Spirit's character (Galatians 5:22; John 7:38, 39) will be cut off until the sin is confessed.

longing for greener pastures

Many of us don't experience the joy of God because we're yearning for someone else's life. Instead of rejoicing in our gift, we look at another's gift, compare it with ours, and end up discouraged.

The individual who is constantly apologizing for his limitations has a faulty view of God's purpose in his life. Perhaps you've always wanted to sing, but you're a monotone. Maybe you'd like to be a leader, but no one wants to follow. Or you've always admired arts and crafts, but when you make any attempt at creativity, the competition of a ten-year-old is too great.

At times like these you have a choice. You can become discouraged and bitter toward God for not supplying a particular gift. Or you can thank God for those who have those gifts. You can enjoy the gifts of others, and praise God for the gifts he's given you. Don't be surprised if others wish they had what you possess.

God has called you to a ministry for which you don't need

another person's gift. You don't need the gift of teaching if he's called you to be a mechanic, but you'd better have the gift of craftsmanship. You don't need the gift of music if God has called you to work in a hospital, but the gift of showing mercy or the gift of healing by medical means is indispensable.

Rejoice in the Lord always. Even when you don't possess some other person's gift. Rejoice, for he has given you all you need to fulfill the task to which he has called you.

JOY CAN BE YOUR EXPERIENCE

Though joy is not everyone's experience, it can be yours. You possess the Holy Spirit. You have his character, and his character is *joy*. I know you want to be able to rejoice, even when everything goes wrong. Besides recognizing the above hindrances to personal joy, you should concentrate on three more positive areas.

focus on the product rather than the process

This procedure is critical, especially when the circumstances are bad. You may be overweight. You've tried all the diets. You've gone on various exercise programs. But you're still having a weight problem. Why? One possible reason is that you're focusing on the process rather than the product. You concentrate too much on the sacrifices you have to make while all your friends enjoy desserts or that buttered sweet roll that activates the salivary glands. You convince yourself, "I haven't had anything good to eat for weeks. I should reward myself with a piece of pie." You know the rest of the story. Temporary pleasure replaces lasting joy.

Or the car is giving us problems. When we arrive at work the boss chews us out for something we didn't do. When we get home we discover an overdue bill we thought was paid. In going through our checkbook we notice an unrecorded $150 check, which means some checks are bouncing. At the moment it seems impossible to rejoice. All we can see are the problems, and none of them provides motivation for rejoicing. The Scriptures encourage us to look beyond the process.

James spoke of a potential chain reaction when problems appear. "The testing of your faith produces endurance. And let endurance have its perfect result, that you may be perfect [mature] and complete, lacking in nothing" (James 1:3, 4). Paul offers a similar concept: "... knowing that tribulation brings about perseverance; and perseverance, proven character; and proven character, hope; and hope does not disappoint" (Romans 5:3-5).

You want to develop your character. You desire to become spiritually mature. Then rejoice when you face difficulties. God uses difficulties to help you understand your deficiencies and his adequacy. Some problems will reveal that you lack patience. Other problems may expose your lack of love, gentleness, or self-discipline. Rejoice! God is not finished with you. He is carving out a beautiful person. Allow him to continue his masterpiece. Cooperate with him. Look at the product (mature character) rather than the process (testing, problems, negative circumstances).

focus on what God is doing in other lives

Do you know how to tell a good teacher from a mediocre one? Discover what gets him excited. My older son had a fifth grade teacher who was outstanding.

Each day Ricky would come home genuinely excited about his schoolwork. He was interested in math, spelling, reading, everything. All I heard for weeks was, "Mr. Boyd said ..." "Mr. Boyd is going to ..." "Mr. Boyd wants the class to ..."

Well, I couldn't wait to meet this Mr. Boyd. When I did, as soon as I introduced myself to him, Mr. Boyd was off and running. He carried the conversation, but he wasn't talking about himself. He was enthusiastically telling me what my son was accomplishing. He almost had me believing that to him Ricky was the most important child in the class. Mr. Boyd was excited about both class achievements and individual accomplishments. He was vitally interested in what was happening in the lives of others.

The early apostles were like that. In spite of all the problems Paul faced (2 Corinthians 11), he refused to wallow in self-pity. Read his epistles. You'll discover that he spent very little time talking about his accomplishments. Most of his letters tell what God was doing in the lives of other believers. To the Thessalonian Christians Paul wrote, "We give thanks to God always for all of you, making mention of you in our prayers; constantly bearing in mind *your* work of faith and labor of love and steadfastness of hope" (1 Thessalonians 1:2-3a).

The Apostle John got excited about the spiritual progress that some of his friends were making. "I have no greater joy than this, to hear of my children walking in the truth" (3 John 4).

Has a friend of yours recently accepted Jesus Christ as Savior? Has a Christian friend returned to a useful life for God? Do you see some beautiful changes taking place in the lives of others? Rejoice! In spite of your current problems, God's blessing in others' lives is evidence that he is alive. He blesses.

focus on God

When our thoughts are glued to our problems we sense limitation and defeat. But when we look to God, limitations fade.

Begin to *center your thoughts on God as the one who is in control of the circumstances.* That may be difficult to swallow at first, but think about it. It's true. Take it by faith. God is in control.

Did you ever desperately want to accomplish something, but when you were about to achieve it, the roof caved in? How did you react? With anger? The panic button? Discouragement?

The Apostle Paul faced that problem. He wanted to reach entire cities for Christ, the man on the street and the man in the palace. But what happened? He got thrown into prison. His goals seemed impossible. How could he preach, locked up in jail? To make matters worse, the Christians themselves were afraid to speak up for the faith.

The Scriptures have preserved Paul's reaction. He rejoiced. He was thrilled about his imprisonment. "And I want you to know this, dear brothers: Everything that has happened to me here has been a great boost in getting out the Good News concerning

Christ. For everyone around here, including all the soldiers over at the barracks, knows that I am in chains simply because I am a Christian. And because of my imprisonment many of the Christians here seem to have lost their fear of chains! Somehow my patience has encouraged them and they have become more and more bold in telling others about Christ ... Christ is being preached and I am glad. I am going to keep on being glad, for I know that as you pray for me, and as the Holy Spirit helps me, this is all going to turn out for my good ... And all the other Christians here want to be remembered to you, especially those who work in Caesar's palace" (Philippians 1:12-14, 18, 19; 4:22, TLB).

Paul knew that God was in control, and as he observed the facts from God's perspective, he realized that his goals were being achieved. Other Christians took up their responsibility to proclaim Christ. The gospel penetrated society and even reached the palace. Mission accomplished. The Bible declares, "Delight yourself in the Lord; and He will give you the desires of your heart" (Psalm 37:4).

Another way to focus on God is to *recognize the value of walking with him.* God makes a promise to those who put him first in life. "In whatever he does, he prospers" (Psalm 1:3). Whatever gift you possess, God will prosper its use.

If you possess the gift of evangelism, you'll introduce others to Jesus. If teaching, you'll see spiritual growth in your students. When you exhort, people will be encouraged. When you help, they will be grateful. If you use your gift of music, focusing on God, people will be moved to praise God.

A third way to concentrate on the Lord is to *give him everything.* The Bible tells us that he gave us all we have. If we are greedy about our possessions, and our possessions are removed, joy vanishes. Joy comes when we give everything back to God, recognizing that we are administrators of his provisions.

This includes our house, car, furniture, health, job, family, education, etc. As long as we hold on to them tightly, joy is conditional (that is, we are joyful if our possessions remain intact). When we release all rights to ownership, then God is responsible for what happens to our possessions.

I shared this idea with a friend who was having difficulty with his lawn. He was constantly irritated because no matter what he did, the bugs kept killing it. He decided to give his lawn back to God. One day I asked, "How is God doing with his lawn?"

"A lot better than I was doing with it," he replied. "It's amazing. The grass is growing again. And what's more amazing is that I'm no longer frustrated over the areas that are still brown. I'm still taking care of it the best I know how, but now God is responsible to make it green."

Attitudes play a large part in our joy or lack of it. Once you give everything back to God and allow him to handle the problems and the blessings, your attitude will change. Rather than focusing on your inadequacy, you'll experience his sufficiency.

Are you rejoicing right now? You can. Whatever problem you face, recognize it as part of God's process to make you a better person. If you question that God is still working miracles, look around. Notice what he is doing in the lives of others. Then set your focus on him. He is in control. He prospers those who walk with him. He will care for everything you give to him.

getting a good night's sleep

Chicago, Minneapolis, or Dallas would have taken it in stride. But an all-night thunder and lightning storm breaking loose in the sunny city of Fresno, California, made the natives extremely restless. No one slept well that night. Children scrambled frantically into their parents' beds. Lonely wives, isolated by a husband's business trip, clutched a pillow for protection. One teen-ager confided, "I thought it was the end of the world." And husbands consoling their wives nervously grinned, "It's just like a woman to get worked up over a little storm."

An unusual storm isn't the only cause of sleepless nights. For certain individuals, insomnia has become a way of life.

The Apostle Paul was no exception. He told the Corinthian church that he experienced "many sleepless nights" (2 Corinthians 11:27). Why? Probably among other things was "the daily pressure upon me of concern for all the churches" (11:28).

The Philippians had a personality problem (Philippians 4:2). The Galatians and Colossians were confronted with false teachers (Judaizers and Gnostics). The Thessalonians faced severe persecution. The Ephesians wrestled with the old self. The Romans abused their liberty in Christ. The Corinthians were plagued with all sorts of problems ranging from immorality to denial of the resurrection of the dead.

What about churches today? Peace becomes an impossible dream when certain individuals use their liberty to fulfill selfish

75

desires. Peace disintegrates when one member threatens another or personality conflicts arise. Rather than seek peace, some pursue war. And one weapon of warfare may be a man's spiritual gift. With his spiritual gift he may destroy peace in his own life, his home life, and his church life.

This is why spiritual character is so important. Even though spiritual gifts don't guarantee peace, the character of God can govern use of our gifts in peace and for peaceful purposes. The fruit of the Spirit is peace. This peace must be integrated with our spiritual gifts.

SPIRITUAL GIFTS AND PERSONAL PEACE

Moses had blown his chance at the Israeli *Who's Who* forty years earlier. Nobility, fame, power, and an unlimited future had vanished with his deadly blow to that Egyptian's head (Exodus 2:12). Now he'd spent the past forty years in the desert grazing sheep, when without warning a voice called out to him, "Moses, Moses! ... I have surely seen the affliction of My people who are in Egypt ... So I have come down to deliver them from the power of the Egyptians ... Therefore, come now, and I will send you to Pharaoh, so that you may bring My people the sons of Israel, out of Egypt" (Exodus 3:4, 7, 8, 10).

God had gifted Moses with leadership ability, but the only leading Moses had done for years was confined to wandering sheep. Moses' first reaction to the offer, put in modern slang, was something like, "You've gotta be kidding! Why didn't you call me forty years earlier when I was somebody? People respected me then. They looked up to me. I had plenty of self-confidence. But now! There's no way I can go down to Egypt and lead a bunch of slaves out from under Pharaoh's nose." Moses had a gift, but he had no peace when he was challenged to use it for the Lord.

Most of us can identify with Moses. Though we're gifted in some ways we find it disturbing to use our gifts for the Lord. We may react with shock, "Who am *I*?" (Exodus 3:11). We may say we just don't know enough about the job to do it well (3:13).

Then we think about all the things that may go wrong (4:1). We try to make it very clear why we aren't qualified (4:10). Finally, we admit that we'd honestly rather not do it because someone else could do it better (4:13).

Must we always go through this process when asked to serve the Lord? Is there no way in which you and I can experience personal peace when an opportunity arises to use our spiritual gift? Here are some principles to put into practice.

be certain that you know the Lord

A God-given ability is no guarantee that an individual has experienced the new birth. A person may be a gifted musician without acknowledging his need of Jesus Christ. He may be eloquent in speech and yet blaspheme the name of the one who gave him the eloquence (Exodus 4:10, 11). If you've never accepted Jesus Christ as your personal Savior, peace will elude you. The Bible declares, "So now, since we have been made right in God's sight by faith in his promises, we can have real peace with him because of what Jesus Christ our Lord has done for us" (Romans 5:1, TLB). Without Christ in your life you remain separated from the one who gave you your gift, and you become burdened with guilt. Where guilt rules, peace cannot enter.

But here's good news. You can be freed from sin and guilt by accepting the payment Jesus made for you. He took your rap. You and I deserved death for our sins, but Jesus died in our place. God is satisfied with that payment for sin. The debt is cancelled. The Scriptures inform us that God "blotted out the charges proved against you, the list of his commandments which you had not obeyed. He took this list of sins and destroyed it by nailing it to Christ's cross" (Colossians 2:14, TLB).

If you would like to experience God's forgiveness, it is yours for the asking. The one condition is to confess to God that you have sinned against him and that you are accepting his Son's payment for your sin.

There is another problem to face, however. Peace with God does not mean that every believer is going to experience the peace of God when he is asked to use his gift. Even the Apostle

Paul knew what it was like to confront a new challenge with fear and trembling (1 Corinthians 2:3).

recognize that God equips you for his service

God will never ask you to accept a work for which he has not equipped you. It would be foolish for me to expect my ten-and eleven-year-old sons to do the work of grown men. But I do expect them to clean their rooms, take out the garbage, and perform other household tasks suitable to their abilities (though not necessarily to their liking).

The military, the government, schools, and churches may bear the reputation of putting the wrong people in the right places, but God does not share that stupidity. The Bible makes it clear that we are not all suited for the same task. "Is everyone an apostle? Of course not. Is everyone a preacher? No. Are all teachers? Does everyone have the power to do miracles? Can everyone heal the sick? Of course not. Does God give all of us the ability to speak in languages we've never learned? Can just anyone understand and translate what those are saying who have that gift of foreign speech?" (1 Corinthians 12:29, 30, TLB).

It is important for you to discover your gift(s). For information on how to discover your gift(s) see chapter 11 of my earlier book, *Discover Your Spiritual Gift and Use It.* Once you begin to understand the equipment God has given you, make yourself available to opportunities where that gift can be used.

Moses claimed that he was not eloquent, but God told him that he was equipped to speak and then promised to speak through him (Exodus 4:10-12). If God has not equipped you musically, don't feel forced to sing in the choir in order to fill the ranks. If you have no concept of how to organize and motivate people to action, don't volunteer to be a leader just because there's a vacancy (unless it's a very temporary situation). Don't run away from any new challenge, but do consider the equipment God has given you and accept tasks suited to your gift(s).

recognize that God gives the increase

Churches today are plagued with the "numbers racket." How

many baptisms? How many new members? By how much did you raise the budget? How many new programs did you add to your Christian education outreach? Then as soon as we collect all the statistics we're supposed to send them to denominational headquarters and compare ourselves with the rest of the denomination. Or if we're an independent church we look around the city and pride ourselves for the number of sheep we've gleaned from the big denominations.

Obviously, a church has to grow if it's alive. I am challenged by church growth seminars. We should learn everything we can about the principles of sowing and reaping for the greatest harvest. But where we have to draw the line is in the area of unhealthy competition and comparison. It is ridiculous to compare the growth rate of a suburban church located in a beautiful, growing area with that of a country church surrounded by acres of cow pasture and near a town of 1,500 with ten other churches.

Over the years many pastors have developed an oversized inferiority complex, and the disease spreads into their churches. Small churches continue to think small and expect little, because they can't compete with their big relatives. The question is not "How big do we want to grow?" Nor is it "How big must we get to win the contest?" We must stop comparing ourselves to our denominational brothers and local neighbors and begin to measure our growth by the opportunities at hand.

Begin to ask, Why has God placed us in this location at this time? Who needs to be reached that no other church is reaching? Who needs to be counseled? Who needs encouragement? Who needs to be visited? Who needs the Savior? Who is being neglected by everyone else? Begin to answer those questions and claim these people for the Lord. Then you will experience both spiritual and numerical growth in your church. Further, design your methods around the needs of the people you're reaching.

If you're in a farm community, you may attempt some form of agricultural program in the church, a kind of Christian 4-H club. If you're in the inner city and ministering to minority groups, you might plan to develop certain skills. Look for those in the congregation who are gifted in craftsmanship. Or begin a bus ministry and employ those with the gift of helps as drivers. Perhaps your church is located near a university. The gift of teaching will probably be more available to your congregation than if you were elsewhere.

Methods differ. You may have more of one gift than another in your congregation because of the type of people who attend. You will also have a different rate of growth. This variety has already been mentioned in Scripture: "Now God gives us many kinds of special *abilities,* but it is the same Holy Spirit who is the source of them all. There are different kinds of *service* to God, but it is the same Lord we are serving. There are many *ways* in which God works in our lives, but it is the same God who does the work in and through all of us who are his" (1 Corinthians 12:4-6, TLB). But whatever ability, whatever service, and whatever method you use to reach people for Christ, remember that blessing and growth come from God.

Paul rebuked the Corinthian believers for comparing one group of believers with another and explained how foolish it was. "Who am I, and who is Apollos, that we should be the cause of a quarrel? Why, we're just God's servants, each of us with certain special abilities, and with our help you believed. My work was to plant the seed in your hearts, and Apollos' work was to water it, but it was God, not we, who made the garden grow in your hearts. The person who does the planting or watering isn't very important, but God is important because he is the one who makes things grow. Apollos and I are working as a team, with the same aim, though each of us will be rewarded for his own hard work" (1 Corinthians 3:5-8, TLB).

Thank God that he will never hold you responsible to do the work of another church or another person. He will reward you for doing what he has called you to do. He will bless you as you are faithful in performing the assignments he gives you. Whether that blessing is greater or smaller than another's is immaterial.

keep the needs of the people in focus

Too often we confuse our objectives with God's purposes. God's purpose for giving us spiritual gifts is to meet the needs of others. We agree with this in theory, but in practice we may have other motives.

Why do our knees knock when we're asked to do something in public? Why does our stomach quiver and our throat tighten? Why do we break out in a cold sweat? Because we feel compassion for people and we're afraid we won't be able to help them? Let's admit that the number one issue at that moment is how we're going to appear in the eyes of others.

Preachers have this problem as well, but I've discovered how to minimize it. Whenever I begin to experience that nervous twitch, the queasy stomach, or the cold sweat, I focus on the needs of the people to whom I'm ministering. In fact, I have nerve enough to write a book only because I'm convinced that thousands of Christians need spiritual character to govern their spiritual gifts. If I weren't persuaded of the need, I'd find some other way to use my time.

saturate yourself with God's Word

The prophet Isaiah wrote many years ago, "Thou wilt keep him in perfect peace, whose mind is stayed on thee: because he trusteth in thee" (Isaiah 26:3, KJV). The psalmist confirmed that testimony: "Those who love Thy law have great peace, and nothing causes them to stumble" (Psalm 119:165).

This truth is especially significant to those who are gifted in preaching, teaching, evangelism, or exhortation. These gifts in particular are dependent upon firsthand knowledge of God's Word. A subtle temptation faces such individuals, however. The ministerial student studies the Bible from many perspectives. He takes Hebrew and Greek to understand the original languages. He spends hours learning Old Testament history. He studies the prophets, the Gospels, and the epistles, often with the purpose of passing future exams.

The temptation is to begin seeing the Bible as a textbook rather than the life-changing revelation of God, able to make the reader "wise unto salvation" and to equip him for God's service (2 Timothy 3:16, 17). It becomes a book of history, language, and facts to remember for the final.

A preacher may view the Scriptures as a supply house for sermons. A teacher may limit his study to, "This is what my class needs. I can't wait to tell them how to live!" An evangelist may never get past John 3:16 and the "milk of the Word" for his own life. The verses memorized and quoted by an exhorter to those he counsels may lose reality for himself.

On the other hand, a craftsman may think, "Why should I study the Bible? I'll never have to teach it. Besides, it's not that important in my line of work." A leader may begin to look to organization as the answer to all problems. One who shows mercy may feel that since he spends so much time in meeting the needs of the handicapped, God won't require any Bible study from him.

No individual is exempt from reading, meditating on, obeying, and sharing God's Word. The person who knows God's Word from firsthand encounter is far better prepared to meet the spiritual needs of others than one who is highly gifted but slack in his personal study.

God promises to bless his Word. "For as the rain and the snow come down from heaven, and do not return there without watering the earth, and making it bear and sprout, and furnishing seed to the sower and bread to the eater; so shall My word be which goes forth from My mouth; it shall not return to Me empty, without accomplishing what I desire, and without succeeding in the matter for which I sent it" (Isaiah 55:10, 11).

God promises to bless those who allow the Word to saturate their lives. "The whole Bible was given to us by inspiration from God and is useful to teach us what is true and to make us realize what is wrong in our lives; it straightens us out and helps us do what is right. It is God's way of making us well prepared at every point, fully equipped to do good to everyone" (2 Timothy 3:16, 17, TLB). Don't allow Satan to delude you into thinking that you can use your spiritual gifts and be filled with peace, while neglecting God's Word.

pray continuously

Most of us are success-oriented in one way or another. No one enjoys failing. Everybody wants to be a winner. But God would do us a disservice if he allowed us always to be successful in everything we attempted.

When we have repeated opportunities to serve the Lord, we begin to worry. "Will I be as good as the last time? Will people like what I do for them? I wonder if they'll accept me again. I hope nothing goes wrong. Will I have enough time? I don't think I'll be able to do it this time." Or if worry doesn't get to us, another temptation may. Ever depend upon past success for future success? It goes something like this. "Oh, this shouldn't be difficult. The last time I tried it the people really liked it. I guess I know the formula. Nothing to worry about. I'll just do exactly as I did the last time and everything should go great." The result?

Picking up the pieces of your shattered pride, you ask, "What'd I do wrong? Why didn't the people respond like the last time?" The answer is that the situation was not identical to the last time. The externals may have been similar. But think back on the last time. Remember how you committed the entire situation into the Lord's hands? Do you recall your attitude of dependence upon his Holy Spirit to work in the lives of the people? It wasn't the gift. Nor was it the personality. God declares, "Not by might, nor by power, but by my Spirit, says the Lord of Hosts—you will succeed because of my Spirit, though you are few and weak" (Zechariah 4:6, TLB).

If you want God's peace to prevail in your life the next time you're asked to get involved, then pray.

Acknowledge that your spiritual gift is from God (1 Corinthians 4:7). This helps remove pride from your heart.

Thank God that he has given you his character (Philippians 2:13). You will then be encouraged that some spiritual benefit can result.

Thank him for his control of circumstances. You can be assured that whether things go wrong (not according to your plan) or right (according to your plan), people will be blessed and God will be glorified.

Thank him that he has promised to meet the needs of people. This moves the responsibility from your limited capacity to his limitless resources and ability.

Ask God to receive the glory from your service, and really mean it. Jesus said, "By this is my Father glorified, that you bear much fruit" (John 15:8a).

Finally, ask God to help you to relax in his Holy Spirit.

You'll be amazed with the results. Peace? Yes. Peace that goes beyond your imagination. No more depending on past success, the power of the flesh, the ingenuity of human wisdom, or the manipulation of people in order to succeed. Worries about being accepted and approved by others will begin to disappear. This type of praying will change you as well as others.

Paul described such prayer when he encouraged the Philippian believers, "Don't worry about anything; instead, pray about everything; tell God your needs and don't forget to thank him for his answers. *If you do this you will experience God's peace,* which is far more wonderful than the human mind can understand. His peace will keep your thoughts and your hearts quiet and at rest as you trust in Christ Jesus" (Philippians 4:6, 7, TLB).

What else could you ask for? Instead of your heart pounding as though it were about to break through your chest, it will be quiet and at rest. Instead of your thoughts dashing off into the realm of possible failure and embarrassment, they will be focused on the one who is going to meet the needs of people, receive the glory, and make you fruitful.

practice what you already know of God's will

Until God's will becomes a way of life with you, peace will be a hit or miss proposition. "Keep putting into practice all you learned from me and saw me doing, and the God of peace will be with you" (Philippians 4:9, TLB).

We may be using our spiritual gift for the Lord. But if we are griping or threatening or full of pride, we cannot expect God's peace to fill our lives.

God's will is expressed in hundreds of commands and exhortations throughout Scripture. As we accept these expressions of God's will and put them into practice when we use our gifts, God's peace will become a reality.

SPIRITUAL GIFTS AND PEACE
IN THE BODY OF CHRIST

Spiritual gifts do not automatically bring peace to the local church. Some gifted teachers become extremely dogmatic. Like the Pharisees they "strain out a gnat and swallow a camel" (Matthew 23:24). Some who use tongues proclaim, "All must have it. Unless you have it you cannot be spiritual." Some even declare, "Unless you've spoken in tongues you can't be a Christian." Gifted musicians may fuss over how a certain number should be sung, or over who's going to get the leading part. Some gifted with exhortation may do a lot of rebuking without having all the facts. Any gift can be used in a way that produces disharmony and discontent instead of peace.

Biblical exhortations to maintain peace in the Body are abundant. "Let us pursue the things which make for peace and the building up of one another" (Romans 14:19). "And let the peace of Christ rule in your hearts, to which indeed you were called in one body; and be thankful" (Colossians 3:15). "Now flee from youthful lusts, and pursue righteousness, faith, love and peace, with those who call on the Lord from a pure heart" (2 Timothy 2:22). The following principles may help us achieve peace.

keep in mind Body function

In some local churches Body function seems to be the responsibility of the "super saints." Statistics indicate that in many churches 20 percent of the people do 80 percent of the work. Imagine the problems you'd face if only 20 percent of your physical body were functioning. Is it any wonder that so many churches perform like invalids? It's because they are.

God never intended that the pastor do the work while the majority of the members sit on the sidelines cheering or booing. Body function includes 100 percent of the body members. Paul wrote, "Under his [Christ's] direction the whole body is fitted together perfectly, and each part in its own special way helps the other parts, so that the whole body is healthy and growing and full of love" (Ephesians 4:16, TLB). Just as your mind tells your hand to scratch when you itch, and signals your legs and feet to cooperate so you can walk, Christ gives commands to the entire Body to function properly.

As Paul expressed it 2,000 years ago, "Suppose the whole body were an eye—then how would you hear? Or if your whole body were just one big ear, how could you smell anything? But that isn't the way God has made us. He has made many parts for our bodies and has put each part just where he wants it. What a strange thing a body would be if it had only one part! So he has made many parts, but still there is only one body. The eye can never say to the hand, 'I don't need you.' The head can't say to the feet, 'I don't need you'" (1 Corinthians 12:17-21, TLB).

As long as a certain group in the church does most of the work, there will be hard feelings, jealousy, self-pity, complaints, and criticisms. When the entire membership begins to use their gifts for the glory of God and the edification of the Body, peace is possible.

But what if there aren't enough jobs to go around? For instance, if you happen to be a member of a 2,000- or 5,000-member church, it's obvious that there won't be several thousand classes to teach. And the choir may be large enough already.

Perhaps the Lord will direct you to begin an entirely new ministry in the church: to the handicapped, or to specific professional or labor groups. It might include beginning a music school. Or you might want to train a group of boys or housewives in a basic mechanics program. If you take spiritual gifts seriously and are convinced that the church should help its individual members develop their gifts, you have a lot of room for creative programs. Too often we send our youth to ungodly musicians and then after a period of several years wonder why they're playing in dance bands and night clubs rather than in the church. We say that God has given the gift, we encourage our members to use their gift, but we ask the world to develop it. I am not advocating that we substitute a skills program for the preaching of the Word. Evangelism and edification must always be the basic objectives of the church. But edification isn't limited to the building up of spiritual life.

A second possibility when you face limited opportunities in your church is to use your gift outside the church building. The gifts are to be used for the entire Body of Christ as well as for reaching the world for Christ. You may be a professor who uses his gift of teaching in a faculty Bible study on campus. You may be a craftsman by gift and a designer or interior decorator by profession. Other churches in your city would greatly profit from your experience and gift. You may advise them or give them free labor in designing or decorating. When I lived in Winnipeg, a gifted craftsman, a contractor by profession, built our gym and educational unit and remodeled our sanctuary at tremendous savings to us. He wasn't a member of our church, but he was committed to using his gifts for the universal Body of Christ.

Your gifts might also be used in Christian schools, publishing houses, hospitals, companies, and in many other areas. Don't neglect your local church. But if the opportunities there are limited, don't neglect your gift.

A third possibility is to use your gift in another church. It's sad to see some large churches with highly gifted individuals warming pews, while smaller churches are crying for workers. Recently a church member came to me and said, "Pastor, you may have wondered where we've been the last two weeks. There's a small struggling church down the street from our house in the country. They really need help, and right now we're trying to decide what to do. We love our church. We've been involved in it for years. But since God has been blessing it so much and so many new people have come, we wonder if he might be able to use us better in the other church." I told him that I admired him for his insight and availability to God. Then I said, "Bill, you'll have to make the final decision. We'll miss you and your wife if you leave. But if you leave here to help a struggling work near your house, you'll go with our blessing and encouragement."

function for the edification of others and the glory of God

We have many reasons for getting involved in the Lord's work. Sometimes it's because no one else will do the job. At times we may feel that our involvement will help us gain favor with God. At other times it's to help us gain a sense of being needed. And sad to say, some just need to show others what they can do.

The Bible tells us that our primary objectives are *(a)* to build up the entire Body of Christ (1 Corinthians 14:4, 12, 26) and *(b)* to bring praise and glory to the one who gave us the gifts (Matthew 5:16).

A question I must continually ask myself as I minister with my gifts is, "Is anyone being helped by what I'm doing?" You've probably evaluated all you were doing at times and concluded that much of it was busywork. No one was helped or built up. No one praised God because of what you were doing. Nobody would miss the work if it were terminated.

If you discover that you no longer have time for your family, check for busywork. If your activity for the Lord is preventing you from spending time with him, consider it a warning signal. If you're beginning to snap at fellow workers and your patience is rapidly dwindling, it's likely that you aren't edifying the saints.

Once each individual begins to use his gift for the edification of the Body and the glory of God, peace will permeate the local Body. Alice won't argue with Barbara that she isn't getting enough solo parts. Instead she will sing to the glory of God and then thank the Lord that he wants to use Caroline next week for the same purpose. Don isn't going to be jealous because they asked Ed to build a pulpit for the front of the church. He knows that he will be able to make something else for God's glory at another time. Fred will thank God for the ten students entrusted to him to teach rather than jealously eyeing Gene's class of forty students.

God never gave us gifts to use for showing off ourselves to one another. If we commit ourselves to that truth, peace will prevail.

encourage peace in the Body

The Bible tells us to "pursue peace with all men" (Hebrews 12:14). Suppose you see a Christian abusing his gift. You can remain silent or you can confront him privately and deal with the problem.

We have a number of college students in our church. God has used them in a powerful way to encourage and challenge the adults in the congregation. The older members can sense the enthusiasm and freshness of these students. But once in a while an over-zealous one decides to straighten out the rest of the Body. When he pursues that task with fervor, peace in the Body is disrupted.

Often the motive of such young zealots is good, but their methods are wrong. Paul warned young Timothy about this problem. "Never speak sharply to an older man, but plead with him respectfully just as though he were your own father. Talk to the younger men as you would to much loved brothers. Treat the older women as mothers, and the girls as your sisters, thinking only pure thoughts about them" (1 Timothy 5:1, 2, TLB). God has called us not to "put down" but to "build up." If you see a gift being used improperly, deal with the issue privately and lovingly.

Another way to pursue peace is to become a "peacemaker." You notice that two members of your church are no longer talking to each other. Instead they have made it a point to talk about each other. You have the choice of sitting back and watching the sparks fly or you can ask God for wisdom as to how best to handle the problem. When such a problem arose in Philippi, Paul handled the situation himself. "And now I want to plead with those two dear women, Euodias and Syntyche. Please, please, with the Lord's help, quarrel no more—be friends again." Then he delegated the responsibility to a friend who was on the scene. "And I ask you, my true teammate, to help these women, for they worked side by side with me in telling the Good News to others; and they worked with Clement, too, and the rest of my fellow workers whose names are written in the Book of Life" (Philippians 4:2, 3, TLB).

The best approach may not be a personal confrontation by yourself. It may involve someone who is closer to the individual than you are. Whatever approach you use, remember that the purpose is to restore a broken relationship and not merely to rebuke the offense. Jesus said, "Blessed are the peacemakers" (Matthew 5:9).

We can have personal peace as we use our spiritual gift. We can experience peace within the Body of Christ as we use our gift. A third area where God wants us to experience peace with our gifts is in the home.

SPIRITUAL GIFTS AND PEACE IN THE HOME

"Home, sweet home" is nothing more than a dream in many family circles. Dad runs down to church for the board meeting. The next night Mother is at her women's meeting. Another evening finds Johnny at his meeting and Jane's is the following night. Rather than complementing the ministry of the home, many churches are competing with it.

Besides programming something for everybody each night of the week, the church has a tendency to place church loyalty above family unity. The mother in the home may be a gifted teacher, but if she runs from one Bible study to another and neglects her family there will be little peace in the home. A well-meaning woman can create a serious barrier between herself and her husband by neglecting him.

How many gifted pastors lose their children? As they pass through the formative years and then the teen years, Dad is too busy to spend time with them. He is full of compassion, but it is poured out on others. He may be a gifted leader, teacher, evangelist, preacher, but his gifts produce bitterness and division in the home rather than love and peace.

Then there is the gifted craftsman or the individual with the gift of helping who spends all his time over at the neighbor's helping him. His wife pleads, "Sam, when are you going to stay home and get some work done around here for a change? Every time the phone rings and someone needs help you're out the door in a minute. But I've been asking you to do these chores for the past three months."

use your spiritual gift in your home

If the Lord has gifted you with teaching, consider your family as your primary classroom. Education began as a family matter.

Moses told his people, "And you must think constantly about these commandments I am giving you today. You must teach them to your children and talk about them when you are at home or out for a walk; at bedtime and the first thing in the morning" (Deuteronomy 6:6, 7, TLB).

Perhaps God has given you the gift of craftsmanship. Does your home reflect that gift? A neighbor several houses up the street has a backyard second to none. When you walk into his yard, you get the feeling that you're up in the Sierras. Mountain plants and rocks garnish the yard. A stream flows from a nearby waterfall and drains into a beautiful pond sporting various breeds of fish. The air is filled with the chirping of birds. Under a large shade tree sits an old shed, equipped with a bed, old iron stove, a few chairs, and other antique paraphernalia. A landscape architect would have charged a fortune to duplicate the scene. But my neighbor used his gift of craftsmanship to accomplish this unique setting at a fraction of the cost.

Another gift that should be used in the home is the gift of leadership. What a waste for an individual who is skilled in organizing and planning to neglect his home. This gift could be used in establishing family budgets. It should definitely be used to manage a family with discipline and direction. One of the qualifications of a church leader is, "He must be one who manages his own household well, keeping his children under control with all dignity (but if a man does not know how to manage his own household, how will he take care of the church of God?)" (1 Timothy 3:4, 5).

maintain God's priorities in the home

Man's first responsibility is not to be at the church preaching, teaching, helping, leading, exhorting, or singing. Nor is his primary role one of going into the world and preaching the gospel to the lost. God holds man responsible for being the head of his home. Paul writes, "But I want you to understand that Christ is the head of every man, and the man is the head of a woman, and God is the head of Christ" (1 Corinthians 11:3). Headship in the Scriptures is not synonymous with dictatorship. God is not saying that the man should be a tyrant over his household. He is saying rather that before the man decides to take care of his neighbors and friends and acquaintances he must care for his family. This means that next to his love for Jesus Christ, he must love his wife, not his church. The preacher who puts his church before his wife's needs may find himself taking his wife to the hospital because of a nervous breakdown. Or he may hear a judge declare, "Divorce granted." I don't mean to say that he should always pamper his wife. But he should be aware of her physical, emotional, intellectual, social, and spiritual needs and meet them as best he can (Ephesians 5:25).

Being the head of the home also means that the husband must provide for the family. "But if anyone does not provide for his own, and especially for those of his household, he has denied the faith, and is worse than an unbeliever" (1 Timothy 5:8). The context indicates that material provision is the primary emphasis. However, a child has the need to be loved, played with, and listened to. Merely providing food for the stomach and clothes for the body is not acting as a responsible head of the home.

The husband-father has a further responsibility as the head of the home. He is responsible to discipline his children (Hebrews 12:9, 10). Managing at the church is of secondary importance (1 Timothy 3:4, 5). Managing down at the office must also take a back seat to home responsibility. As long as the man in the family reverses God's priority system and puts church, job, or his own interests before those of his family, there will be little peace in the home.

Woman's first responsibility is to God. She is responsible to be a God-fearing woman (Proverbs 31:30; Matthew 6:33). Second, the married woman is to be a helper, suited to her husband. "And the Lord God said, 'It isn't good for man to be alone; I will make a companion for him, a helper suited to his needs'" (Genesis 2:18, TLB). Some women will say, "But my husband isn't a Christian. They need me down at the church." Or "The Bible study will fall apart if I'm not there." What are God's priorities for a married woman? She is to be a good wife. "Wives, fit in with your husbands' plans; for then if they refuse to listen when you talk to them about the Lord, they will be won by your respectful, pure behavior. Your godly lives will speak to them better than any words" (1 Peter 3:1, 2, TLB).

A third area of most women's responsibility is to be a mother. In many homes women reverse priorities two and three. Most of their time and interest are with the children. If there is any time, love, or interest left over at the end of the day, they may share some with their husband. Some women have gone this route by default. The husband is never home, so they might as well lavish their love and time on the kids. The big problem begins to show itself when the children leave home. A house that was once filled with a family is now occupied by two strangers. Notice the order given to Titus. "Older women likewise are to be reverent in their behavior ... that they may encourage the young women *(a)* to love their husbands, *(b)* to love their children..." (Titus 2:3, 4). You are a wife first and a mother second.

But what about ministry to others? The Scriptures don't limit the woman to the home. She may have interests of her own (Proverbs 31:16, 20, 24). She may have a ministry to others such as teaching, counseling, visiting, exhorting, singing, etc., but—like the husband—she must not place these interests above the needs of her family. To redesign God's order of priorities is to tamper with your chances for peace in the home.

This truth applies just as much to children in the home. God does not place all responsibility upon the shoulders of parents. Children must share the burden. The Scriptures emphasize two priorities before self-interest. God must be first. Jesus said, "He who loves father or mother more than Me is not worthy of Me" (Matthew 10:37). If a parent were to tell his child to do something that was obviously contrary to the will of God, the child must make a choice. To obey his parent would be to disobey God. To obey God would mean disobeying his parent. Since the great commandment is first to love the Lord and then to love man (Matthew 22:36-39), the child would have to obey God.

But there is a second priority. "Children, obey your parents in the Lord, for this is right. Honor your father and mother (which is the first commandment with a promise)" (Ephesians 6:1, 2). As young children we obey our parents, but as we grow into adult life we honor them. The reason I dedicated my first book to my

Dad was not to obey him. (He hadn't the slightest idea of my intentions.) The dedication was to honor him, to demonstrate in some tangible way how I've felt toward him over the years. Had my mother been living, the dedication would have included her.

A disobedient or dishonoring child brings no peace into a home. "Happy is the man with a level-headed son; sad the mother of a rebel." "A rebellious son is a grief to his father and a bitter blow to his mother" (Proverbs 10:1; 17:25, TLB). In recent years a group called the Children of God has tragically overemphasized the first priority to the complete neglect of the second. Young believers have been forced literally to forsake their parents. Brokenhearted parents have seen their sons and daughters walk out the door, never to return. No correspondence. No communication. This is not Christlikeness. Even at the end, as our Lord hung on the cross, he said to his mother, "Woman, behold, your son! Then he said to the disciple, "Behold, your mother!" "And from that hour the disciple took her into his own household" (John 19:26, 27).

Spiritual gifts don't guarantee peace in our personal life. They won't automatically produce peace in the church or in the home. But they can be used in peace and for peaceful purposes. Being aware of these truths is the first step to experience God's peace. But the next giant step is to pay the price willingly, for peace will be realized only on God's terms, not ours.

CHAPTER SEVEN

I can't wait to be patient

The youth of our society have been called the Now Generation. Whatever the unfulfilled desire, they want it completed *now*. But impatience isn't limited to adolescents. It's a disease that has affected each one of us.

Western culture might be labeled the "Instant Society." We have instant coffee, instant potatoes, instant breakfast, instant pudding, and then we go on an instant diet. We attend church and hope to hear an instant sermon. Some young people are searching for the instant will of God. Those who want to enter professional Christian service (ministry, missionary work, student work, religious music, etc.) are tempted to attend the school promising instant graduation. Six-month and one-year Bible courses are becoming popular. I'm afraid we'll reap spiritual immaturity from the seed we sow.

Recently the medical profession has released information on certain personality types that are more prone to impatience than others. Drs. Meyer Friedman and Ray Rosenman are convinced that a relationship exists between personality traits and heart attacks. They classify people as either "Type A" or "Type B." "At least 90 percent of all patients having heart attacks under age 60, we've found, exhibit a Type A behavior pattern" (Quoted with permission from *The National Observer,* copyright Dow Jones & Company, Inc. 1974. As reprinted in *Reader's Digest,* August 1974, p. 66). The classic Type A personality is described in the

95

same article as *"habitually impatient,* constantly under stress from an urgent, pressing feeling that he hasn't enough time. His body movements are brisk. He speaks in explosive, hurried speech, and his body seems always tense, never relaxed. He is often obsessed with numbers—of sales made, articles written, forms completed—and prone to vent hostility in verbal abuse, even on family or friends" (pp. 66, 67). Need I say that a Christian is not automatically exempt from becoming a Type A personality, with all its consequences?

Whatever your basic personality, however, God has supplied you with the ability to develop patience. If the Holy Spirit dwells within your body (Romans 8:9) you have the potential to become patient. The character of the Holy Spirit is love, joy, peace, patience... (Galatians 5:22). This spiritual quality must be developed along with your spiritual gifts. You can learn to be patient with yourself, with others, and with God.

PATIENCE WITH YOURSELF

Impatience is not a temptation that we first face as teen-agers. It comes with the package, so to speak. The newborn infant is hungry soon after birth. It doesn't wait until the mother feels like feeding. In a split second the infant's stomach sends the message to the brain, "Hey, man, it's empty down here. Sound the alarm!"

The problem continues. When the child makes his first attempts to roll over, to crawl, and to walk, observe the frustrated look on his face as he tries and fails, then tries and fails again.

The Bible describes some similarities in the spiritual realm between ourselves and children. As we were all born physically, so we must all be born spiritually (John 3:3, 7). As we have been given physical potential to grow, so God has given us spiritual potential to develop (1 Corinthians 12:11; Romans 8:9). We experience impatience in discovering, developing, and using our spiritual as well as physical abilities.

be patient while you learn

Take, for instance, the problem of learning about the potential that God has given you for a meaningful spiritual life. You may always have believed that spiritual gifts were only for a spiritual elite. Perhaps you have never contributed much to the cause of Christ because you thought you had nothing to contribute. Now you know that God has gifted you. But you may not yet know what gifts you possess. Where should you begin?

You could first think about those things you do well (see chapter 11 of *Discover Your Spiritual Gift and Use It*). But you should also make yourself available to help wherever help is needed. As you get involved, you will discover what gifts you do and do not possess. You should also get feedback from the pastor or a close friend, who may confirm or question the gift.

Discovery is a rewarding process. Joan has been thrilled over the lessons God has been teaching her. She made her first attempt at teaching several years ago. During her second year Joan recognized that teaching was not her gift. One truth impressed upon her, however, came from Galatians 6:2: "Bear one another's burdens." She immediately thought of her neighbor's marriage problems and determined to claim Janet for Christ. She asked God to open an opportunity to help in a natural and non-threatening way. God answered her prayer several days later. At Joan's invitation, Janet came over for coffee. The Lord had so prepared her heart that she turned the conversation to her marriage problems. Joan was able to show Janet the deeper problem, her lack of a spiritual relationship with Jesus Christ. That afternoon Janet placed her personal faith in Christ. Within a few weeks her husband also found the Savior. Today their marriage is not merely holding together. It has become a beautiful growing relationship with Christ at its center.

That experience caused Joan to think that she might have the gift of evangelism. She thought of other friends with their problems, and now God has used her to introduce many of them to Christ.

be patient while you grow

It is possible to be patient while you *develop your abilities*. Growth is time-consuming. Jesus referred to stages of growth:

"The earth produces crops by itself; first the blade, then the head, then the mature grain in the head" (Mark 4:28). Impatience results from expecting everything to happen at once.

Learn all you can at your present level of growth. Until you master the basics, your use of your gifts will be hampered. (The reason why so few golfers shoot better than 100 is because they've never mastered the basics. I speak from experience.)

Don't let the goal out of your sight. "Brethren, I do not regard myself as having laid hold of it yet; but one thing I do: forgetting what lies behind and reaching forward to what lies ahead, I press on toward the goal for the prize of the upward call of God in Christ Jesus" (Philippians 3:13, 14). What are the possible ways in which God may use you if you develop your gifts? Think of them. Recognize any shortcut you're tempted to take as a potential limitation of the future.

Your perspective of Jesus' return may help you develop your gifts with patience. Some who believe that Jesus is coming soon make a mistake like that of certain Thessalonian believers (2 Thessalonians 3:6-13). The rationalized, "If Jesus is coming soon, it's no use working. We'll just wait for him. And when we get hungry, we'll get some food from another brother." One present-day version: "If Jesus is coming in the near future, I'm not going to waste my time in university, Bible college, or seminary. We've got to save the world. There's no time for that kind of education." What this individual doesn't consider is that he could be an effective witness while attending school. At the same time he can become better equipped there to serve the Lord.

When the Lord does return for his people, he isn't going to count the number of people you've led to Christ. He is interested that you do exactly what he has led you to accomplish. When Jesus described a faithful and wise steward he said, "Blessed is that servant, whom his lord when he cometh shall find so doing" (Luke 12:43, KJV). If God wants you in school and you choose to be out "serving" him instead, it's no feather in your cap. If Jesus finds you in school when he returns, he'll say, "Well done, good and faithful servant. You were doing exactly what I asked you to do."

be patient in your work

A third area in which we need patience with ourselves is when we use the abilities that God has given us. Whenever we serve the Lord, we want to be successful. But problems arise when we want as much success as certain other people or when we want success immediately.

God does not call you to some other person's work, and he therefore won't give you someone else's blessing. When the master in the parable gave out talents he distributed five, two, and one. On the day of reckoning, he expected to receive the results of each person's stewardship in proportion to the amount he had entrusted to him. Just so, God expects from you only in proportion to what he has given you.

"And let us not lose heart in doing good, for in due time we shall reap if we do not grow weary" (Galatians 6:9). Don't give up. You may feel that you're knocking your head against the wall. You pray. You work. You keep waiting for God to do something significant. The Lord's promise to you is, "You will be successful as you continue to serve in my power and for my glory."

PATIENCE WITH OTHERS

Patience with others seems beyond everyone at times. You've made a luncheon appointment for 12 noon. You wait ten, twenty, thirty minutes. Your heart pumps faster, and you tell off your luncheon partner in your mind. How can he be so inconsiderate?

Or perhaps you're working with a slow learner. It might be a student in school or Sunday school, a fellow employee, even one of your own children. No matter how many times you explain the problem, he doesn't seem to grasp it. You ask yourself, "Will he ever grow up? Will he ever learn?"

Almost 2,000 years ago, one of the New Testament writers wrote, "And we urge you, brethren, admonish the unruly, encourage the fainthearted, help the weak, *be patient with all men*" (1 Thessalonians 5:14). Well, that's a start. To know that we should be patient is helpful; it sets the direction. But knowing how to be patient is something else. The Scriptures provide some helpful principles.

remember that other individuals develop at their own pace

After their first missionary journey, Paul and Barnabas had a disagreement (Acts 15:36-41). Barnabas wanted to take John Mark with them on their second trip. Paul refused. Mark had deserted them early in the first expedition (Acts 13:13). Each man argued his point, but neither was able to persuade the other. So Barnabas decided not to travel with Paul, but chose to return to Cyprus. He contacted young Mark and took him back home. In contrast, Paul followed through with his plan to visit the young churches he and Barnabas had established. Together he and Silas traveled through Syria and Cilicia.

Which one was right? Who acted according to the will of God? I believe that both were right. The dispute resulted from a difference in perspective. They each did what they were committed to do, and God blessed them both. In the book of Acts, Luke recorded the events of Paul's second and third missionary journeys (Luke traveled with him). Near the end of his life, in prison, Paul wrote to Timothy, "Only Luke is with me. Pick up Mark and bring him with you, for he is useful to me for service" (2 Timothy 4:11). That was the same kid who had run away when things got rough, but now Paul considered him useful. How did that happen? Well, probably his cousin Barnabas had a hand in helping him mature (Colossians 4:10). And that was the same Mark who eventually wrote the second Gospel.

You may know a potential John Mark right now. He may be full of fear, apprehension, care, or rebellion. He may not catch on at first. He probably doesn't have your perspective or enthusiasm. He may not be developing at the same pace as others his age; he may be immature or frighteningly precocious. But God has equipped him to be useful for service. He may test your patience, but hang in there. God hasn't given up on him.

reflect on what God has done in the lives of others

The Bible is a refreshing reservoir of changed lives. You can read how a vindictive man like John was changed into an apostle of love (Luke 9:51-54). You learn how an impetuous fisherman became a leader of the early church (John 21:15-17; Acts 2:14). And what about your own experience? Remember that kid you thought would never amount to anything? Today God is using him in a remarkable way. Recall the girl with whom you spent hours, trying to help her with all those problems? Now she's being used by God to help others with similar difficulties.

make the most of your time

"Therefore be careful how you walk, not as unwise men, but as wise, making the most of your time, because the days are evil" (Ephesians 5:15, 16). When you and I get impatient waiting for someone, it's more our problem than theirs. Whether they have a legitimate excuse or not, the problem lies with us. It took me a long time to accept this, but once I acknowledged my failure I was able to conquer my impatience of waiting.

What is the real issue? Management of my time. Several years ago a good friend of mine fell into the habit of arriving late. Since I've always been a stickler about getting to appointments on time, I was really disturbed. I tried to solve the problem by making jokes. Then the jokes turned to sarcasm. When that failed, I advanced into the silent treatment. Then I told him how provoked I was getting. Both of us were becoming frustrated. He made several efforts to improve. They proved successful once or twice. But in a few weeks we'd be back to the same old frustration. He was embarrassed. I was angry.

During this period I read several books about time management which emphasized the need to use those "wasted moments" in a more meaningful way. So I decided that every time I made a luncheon appointment with my friend, I would use the waiting time constructively. I replaced frustration with reading, planning, or creative thinking. I carried either a book or a pen and paper. This became a time to solve problems, set priorities, prepare sermons. When I established this habit pattern, my impatience subsided. The first ten minutes of the luncheon were no longer used to melt the ice. We could get down to business immediately.

The application of this principle isn't limited to waiting for a late appointment. The Sunday school teacher who sits under the hair dryer can use that time constructively thinking through lesson plans, praying for her students, reading background information, or deciding how to handle a problem child. The gifted leader can listen to a cassette tape while driving (e.g., on management, working with people, planning, organizing, or other leadership subjects). Proper use of our time will eliminate much of the impatience from our lives.

realize how long it has taken you to get to where you are spiritually

"Consider your calling..." (1 Corinthians 1:26). When God started with you and me he began with raw material: "... not many wise according to the flesh, not many mighty, not many noble; but God has chosen the foolish things of the world ... the weak things ... the base things ... and the despised ... the things that are not ... that no man should boast before God" (1 Corinthians 1:26-29). You may be mature today. But a few years ago, it was a different story.

I vividly recall standing in front of my high school English teacher and hearing him say, "Yohn, you'll never amount to a thing!" With all the facts before him, he was absolutely correct. At that point in my life I hadn't planned to amount to anything, and I was right on target. My problem was direction and motivation. My English teacher's problem was one of impatience, failure to acknowledge the power of God's grace. I was raw material at best. But since God majors in creating order out of chaos, he saw me as just another challenge. Whatever profit I am today, it is because of the grace of God. And whatever problem I am today, I can rest in the fact that God is not through with me yet.

Whenever you have difficulty being patient with some other individual's development, take a good look at yourself a few years ago. Paul wrote, "For I am the least worthy of all the apostles, and I shouldn't even be called an apostle at all after the way I treated the church of God. But whatever I am now it is all because God poured out such kindness and grace upon me" (1 Corinthians 15:9, 10, TLB).

recognize that you don't always know all of the facts

One of the gifts specifically needing patience according to the Scriptures is the gift of exhortation. "Preach the word; be ready in season and out of season; reprove, rebuke, *exhort, with great patience and instruction*" (2 Timothy 4:2). The minister is not the only exhorter in the Body of Christ. Many people are capably gifted in this responsibility, especially lay counselors. Someone comes to you with a problem. It may be a friend, family member, or acquaintance. They share their problem with you. Thinking you have all the necessary information, you advise them to take specific action. A few days later they come back and tell you it didn't work. You can't understand, but as the conversation continues you discover new information that changes the picture completely. Again you advise. This time your friend returns to tell you that the problem is worse. You attempt to mask your surprise. Through further inquiry you learn that your friend actually never took your advice. He was afraid to try because of another part of the problem he just now unveils for you. By this time your patience is wearing thin. But the more he confides in you, the more clearly you understand. You begin to see the picture. Now that you see the pressure your friend is really under, it's easier to have patience with his times of failure.

The leader should keep this principle in mind as he attempts to innovate ideas or programs that have never before been tried. He may at first become impatient with those who don't immediately accept his ideas. When he investigates the background of the resistance, he can better appreciate the fears.

The first year that I came to Fresno I wanted to begin a specific kind of missionary conference that had never been attempted in the church. I knew the exact speaker to launch the program, but when I suggested the idea to our missionary committee it was greeted with suspicion. At the outset I was startled. I couldn't understand how anyone could oppose something that would be so beneficial to so many. Further investigation revealed that the way I presented the idea made it sound as though everything in the past was wrong. I was beginning to see that the problem was not so much the idea as it was my communication of the idea. I therefore determined to "sit on" the suggestion for two more years. Then during my third year as pastor, after the people had more confidence in me as an individual, I presented the idea again. This time there was no problem. The Lord blessed the ministry of the speaker who got the program off the ground in a beautiful fashion. Before you lose patience, get the facts, all of them.

PATIENCE WITH GOD

Here is a third battlefield for patience. Suppose you've been praying that God would bring a relative to himself. Years have passed and your relative still doesn't know the Lord. Your patience with God begins to wane.

Or perhaps you've actually asked God to make you more patient, yet during the past three months life has become more hectic. Pressures are greater. Problems have increased. Your patience with God is rapidly decreasing.

Do we ever lose patience with God? There's no doubt about it. We do. But again, the problem is not with God. It lies in our inability or refusal to accept God for who he is.

For instance, *do you really believe that God is faithful?* "For I am confident of this very thing, that He who began a good work in you will perfect it until the day of Christ Jesus" (Philippians 1:6). God promises. God begins his work. God completes his work.

A popular speaker recently told an audience at Mount Hermon, California, that he had been praying for his father's salvation for forty years. Then he added, "I received a long distance phone call a few months ago. I heard what to me was at first unbelievable. My father had just come to know the Lord." If a thousand years is as one day with the Lord, forty years is a matter of minutes.

Most of us have difficulty waiting forty days, let alone forty years, for a prayer to be answered. We're like the man who planted a tree in his yard. Every second week he would dig it up to see if it was taking root. The Bible declares, "Faithful is He who calls you, and He also will bring it to pass" (1 Thessalonians 5:24).

God works according to his time schedule. The Scriptures speak of "the fullness of time" (Galatians 4:4), "the proper time" (Matthew 24:45), and "due time" (Galatians 6:9). "There is an appointed time for everything. And there is a time for every event under heaven" (Ecclesiastes 3:1). God does not operate haphazardly. He has a schedule which he follows precisely.

At times we attempt to persuade God to abandon his schedule and work within our own. He has no interest in the offer, so we plead, we bargain, we make various promises. If God will do so and so in such a time, then we will.... But God doesn't budge. He has excellent reasons for doing what he does when he does it.

The Lord knows what sequence of events must take place before our desires are fulfilled, and he operates according to that program. If one of the elements were to be neglected, we would lose something important. A young couple who desperately want a happy marriage may put God's order out of sequence. Because of impatience they put sex before marriage. Later they wonder why their marriage is filled with guilt, frigidity, and fears. Fit into God's schedule and you'll begin to experience the fulfillment he wants you to have.

We also become impatient if we feel that the Lord should give us a more public opportunity to use our gifts. We knock ourselves out behind the scenes and everyone else seems to get the credit. We don't exactly want to be a hero, but we wouldn't mind a little recognition now and then. God has an answer for us. "Humble yourselves, therefore, under the mighty hand of God, that *He may exalt you at the proper time*" (1 Peter 5:6). We have to be willing to say, "OK, Lord. I'm going to stop trying for recognition. I have one desire: to serve you. If you want me to become popular or to remain an unknown, it no longer matters. I ask for one thing only: to remain faithful to you in whatever I do."

Nothing is more obnoxious in the Body than brothers or sisters in Christ exalting themselves. One individual always speaks out at Bible studies, meetings, and Sunday school class. Another does most of the praying at prayer meeting. A third always wants to lead. A fourth shows off his ability to sing. They believe that whenever they feel like it is always the "proper time."

God's concept of the proper time is "when we are capable of handling the responsibility." This means not only that we have the ability, but also demonstrate mature character. To go on an ego trip reflects a deficiency in character. If we try to exalt ourselves, our gifts alone will be insufficient to produce spiritual results.

You may not be doing those "great things" for God that you want to do. Your gift may be yet hidden from the public eye. But don't blame God. Don't lose patience. There are significant and necessary changes he wants to make in your life. When you are ready, he will promote you. By that time you may feel like Moses, "Who am I?" But then you'll hear him reply, "Certainly I will be with you" (Exodus 3:12).

James Michener, the Pulitzer Prize-winning author of *South Pacific, Hawaii,* and other popular works, was forty years old before he wrote anything. Michener says he doesn't expect an individual to accomplish anything of great significance until after the age of thirty-five ("On Wasting Time," *Reader's Digest,* October 1974). Moses was eighty when he began his adventure with Pharaoh. John the Apostle was probably in his nineties when he made his contribution to Scripture. Apparently, at least seventeen years passed between the time of Paul's conversion and his most significant accomplishments for Christ (Galatians 1:18; 2:1).

If you are in your early twenties or thirties and feel that God has forgotten you because no one recognizes your gifts, relax. The Lord knows the proper time for you. But you must take the first step: "Humble yourself before him."

Finally, *crave the complete fulfillment of God's will in your life.*

This means that if you are single, marriage is not now God's complete will for you. It may be part of his program. Marriage may seem extremely important, but don't panic. God wants more for your life than a wife or husband. He wants to develop you into a fulfilled person, one who is maturing in character and ability, one who consistently experiences God's blessings.

If you are married, God will use many events from everyday life to mold you into a Christlike person. He may choose the times when your children are sick to teach you to rely on him. He may select those frustrating days when you have no job to teach you that he is the Supplier of every need. He may use the death of a loved one to teach you that he is the Divine Comforter. He may allow you to experience personal failure in order to help you develop humility.

Patience is not a "once for all" spiritual experience. It's a spiritual quality that grows as we put God first in every circumstance. It's an attitude that says: "God, thank you that you control circumstances. I want your will fulfilled in my life as well as in the lives of others. You know the beginning from the end, so I'm willing to wait for you to complete your program in your time."

learning to be kind

Many Americans are attempting to pattern their lives after the "man's man" they see so often on television.

First, he's a man who eventually gets his way. He may have to struggle, demand, threaten, or manipulate, but he gets what he wants. Second, he has a relative concept of morality. Rightness is determined by his desire to have his way. If someone is hurt in the process, tough luck. Third, he uses kindness primarily as a means to an end—and therefore uses it sparingly and discreetly.

The "man's man" is a menace to both the male and the female image. Assertiveness is "where it's at," we hear, a trait expected in men and to be cultivated by women. Kindness is replaced with hardness. Quietness is superseded by giving others a piece of your mind. Humility has had it.

Are adherents of such views in church? Sometimes in abundance. Helen, for instance, is quick-tempered. She knows how to put people in their place. She uses sarcasm to shred her victim. She keeps track of the strengths and weaknesses of each member. Of course, as long as you don't cross her, she's a "lovely" person. But accidentally step on her toes and "Shazam!" She turns supersour.

Irene isn't so violent as Helen, but she's just as vicious. Her thing is character assassination. She maintains a daily hot-line into the homes of the church's self-appointed CIA. When Irene discovers a scandalous piece of news she immediately shares the blessing, usually on a spiritual basis. "Jane, please don't tell anyone else, but I've just heard that Katie's husband ... I just wanted you to know so that you could pray more intelligently."

And then there's Louise. She preaches to her friends. "Don't be so kind and submissive to your husband. You'll spoil him. He'll take advantage of you. You're lowering your image. You're hindering the cause of womanhood! We need women on the church boards. Let's elect women elders. Let's put the men in their place!"

And Max is no better. He scares people into performing for him. He uses threats and a nasty temper to get his way. He may be the heir to the family throne, and since his father and grandfather were chairmen of the board, he thinks he has a right to the position. If Max is the church's money man, he may use his money as power. As long as everything goes his way, he gives systematically. But when the church balks at his suggestions, he's prepared to leave and take his money with him.

Ned is another unkind member. There's only one way to get anything done around the church: his way. He sees compromise as weakness. "I'm a deacon. If I change my mind and go along with the majority, I'll lose my authority. Let them change!"

Otto differs from the other types of unkind people in that he isn't aggressively unkind. He has no violent temper. He doesn't demand his way. He isn't a gossip, or an activist for any cause. He just refuses to get involved. He can see all kinds of needs in front of his eyes and yet turn his back.

Is it possible that a trace of unkindness weaves itself through your inner life? Has your wife ever commented, "Honey, you sounded so rough when you talked with the kids. Would you try to be a little more tender?" Or has your husband said lately, "You behave so standoffish when you're around Pat. She's always friendly to you. Why are you so rude to her?" Sometimes we're unkind to each other without knowing it. At other times we're deliberately unkind.

Spiritual gifts can complicate the problem. Even in the Bible, some people misused their gifts. Gifts of teaching, leadership, prophecy, etc., were sometimes used in ways bereft of kindness.

GIFTS WITHOUT KINDNESS

the gift of teaching

The Pharisees of Jesus' day were noted teachers. They spent hours studying the laws and traditions of the fathers. In fact, by the time our Lord came to earth, these religious teachers had tragically mixed up the laws of God with the traditions of men. No one knew where the one began and the other left off.

The Pharisees used their teaching as a tool to get others to conform to their way of life. This caused them to develop calloused hearts. One such incident is presented in Mark 3:1-6. "And He [Jesus] entered again into a synagogue; and a man was there with a withered hand. And they were watching Him to see if He would heal him on the Sabbath, in order that they might accuse Him. And He said to the man with the withered hand, 'Rise and come forward!' And He said to them, 'Is it lawful on the Sabbath to do good or to do harm, to save a life or to kill?' But they kept silent. And after looking around at them with anger, grieved at their hardness of heart, He said to the man, 'Stretch out your hand.' And he stretched it out, and his hand was restored. And the Pharisees went out and immediately began taking counsel with the Herodians against Him, as to how they might destroy Him."

The Pharisees had no concern for the man's need. Kindness did not enter into their response. They were angry because Jesus wasn't conforming to their teaching and life style. Today we have teachers in the church who operate on the same premise. They may teach that loyalty to the local church or denomination is identical with loyalty to Jesus Christ. To leave "our" group for another is the same as leaving the "faith once delivered to the saints."

Some groups today proclaim that they are the only real New Testament disciples. They may use the gift of teaching to bind their followers through long lists of rules and regulations. Those who don't conform are criticized, ostracized, or publicly humiliated.

The gift of teaching can edify, but it also can be used unkindly.

the gift of leadership or administration

This gift is used unkindly when a leader dominates others. Diotrephes was a leader in one of the New Testament churches. It's not clear whether he was a pastor, board chairman, or what. But the Apostle John describes his use of leadership in the third letter. "I sent a brief letter to the church about this, but proud Diotrephes, who loves to push himself forward as the leader of the Christians there, does not admit my authority over him and refuses to listen to me. When I come I will tell you some of the things he is doing and what wicked things he is saying about me and what insulting language he is using. He not only refuses to welcome the missionary travelers himself, but tells others not to, and when they do he tries to put them out of the church" (3 John 9, 10, TLB). Diotrephes sounds like some church leaders today—self-seeking, loving position and power. Leadership used in this manner divides believers and dishonors God.

the gift of prophecy

What prophet used his gift grudgingly? You guessed it—Jonah. From the beginning he didn't want to carry God's message to Nineveh, and even after his voyage in God's special "submarine," Jonah was a bitter man. He walked the city streets announcing that doomsday was just forty days away. When the people repented, what was Jonah's reaction? He complained to God. "This is exactly what I thought you'd do, Lord, when I was there in my own country and you first told me to come here. That's why I ran away to Tarshish. For I knew you were a gracious God, merciful, slow to get angry, and full of kindness; I knew how easily you could cancel your plans for destroying these people" (Jonah 4:2, TLB). What a contrast between Jonah—bitter and angry—and God—compassionate and kind.

Jonah wanted to use his gift of prophecy to get even with the Assyrians, to bring fear and a sense of hopelessness into their lives. He wanted to use his gift to make them sweat it out until the axe fell.

Jonah reminds me of some preachers today who really get a

kick out of dangling people over the pit. Some pastors use the pulpit as a means of getting even with their critics. Others use it to sweep away opposition to their proposals. Some degrade those who fail to show up at all of the church meetings and services. In many churches, kindness is missing from the pulpit.

Enough of the problem. What about the solution? How can we let kindness govern our spiritual gifts?

GIFTS WITH KINDNESS

place the needs of others above your interests

To put others first, it's obvious that we must rely on the empowering of the Holy Spirit. We are born into the world self-centered. In our early years we're the center of everyone's attention, so it's unnatural for us to lay aside our interests for someone else—especially outside our immediate family.

Sometimes meeting the needs of others challenges our security. It may mean leaving home, changing jobs, or giving up our comfortable standard of living. Our physical safety may be endangered. We may have to share, sacrifice, become vulnerable.

The Apostle Paul described various responses to such challenges when he wrote to the believers in Philippi, "There is no one like Timothy for having a real interest in you; everyone else seems to be worrying about his own plans and not those of Jesus Christ ... Meanwhile, I thought I ought to send Epaphroditus back to you. You sent him to help me in my need; well, he and I have been real brothers, working and battling side by side. Now I am sending him home again, for he has been homesick for all of you and upset because you heard that he was ill. And he surely was; in fact, he almost died ... Welcome him in the Lord with great joy, and show your appreciation, for he risked his life for the work of Christ and was at the point of death while trying to do for me the things you couldn't do because you were far away" (Philippians 2:20, 21, 25-27, 29, 30, TLB).

The gifts of helping and showing mercy would especially lend themselves to this challenge. People seldom need help at a time convenient for us. A neighbor dies suddenly. A friend is in an accident. They need another helper in the church nursery in about half an hour, the very night you decided to stay home and relax. How will you respond?

minister to those whom others have rejected

Barnabas was a gifted exhorter. At times he admonished. At other times he encouraged and comforted. But whenever the Bible describes Barnabas using his God-given ability, we sense his kindness.

Paul was at first rejected by the believers in Jerusalem, but Barnabas introduced and recommended him to the church (Acts 9:26-30). When John Mark was rejected by Paul, Barnabas came to Mark's rescue (Acts 15:36-39).

Today all churches have individuals who feel rejected. No one takes an interest in them, or thinks about inviting them home for a meal after the service. They never receive a personal invitation to a church social. They may be old. They may live alone. Perhaps they're poor, or speak with an accent. Their physical features may be different. Their education could be too much or too little.

Most of us have developed subtle ways of rejecting people. A cold shoulder is what keeps most of the unwanteds from coming back. But more genteel "body language" can also reject visitors—the look of our eyes, inflection in our voices, our handshake, the phoniness of our smile. Instead of looking a person straight in the eyes, we focus on his beard or clothes or hair. We may greet him with a handshake, but be looking around for a friend we're more interested in talking to.

Recently someone told me about the impact a member of our church had on her the first time she visited. "After the service this lady came up to me and introduced herself. As we talked, I got the impression that she was interested in me as a person, not as a visitor. She was genuine. She cared. I knew that if I ever needed help, she'd be the one I'd contact. I really felt accepted for myself."

channel your gift to edify the body, not to demonstrate the gift

Kindness asks, "How can I use my gifts to build up the lives of others?" But many gifted people seldom ask that question. Instead they wonder, "How can I show these people how good I really am?" Or "How can I prove to everyone that I'm spiritual?"

The tongues group in Corinth was asking the wrong question. Some elevated this gift above others. Some used it publicly when there was no one around to interpret, so the Body failed to be enriched. Paul admonished, "But if your gift is that of being able to 'speak in tongues,' that is, to speak in languages you haven't learned, you will be talking to God but not to others, since they won't be able to understand you. You will be speaking by the power of the Spirit but it will all be a secret. But one who prophesies, preaching the messages of God, *is helping others grow in the Lord,* encouraging and comforting them. So a person 'speaking in tongues' helps himself grow spiritually, but one who prophesies, preaching messages from God, *helps the entire church grow* in holiness and happiness ... Since you are so anxious to have special gifts from the Holy Spirit, ask him for the very best, for *those that will be of real help to the whole church* ... Well, my brothers, let's add up what I am saying. When you meet together some will sing, another will teach, or tell some special information God has given him, or speak in an unknown language, or tell what someone else is saying who is speaking in the unknown language, but everything that is done must be *useful to all, and build them up in the Lord*" (1 Corinthians 14:2-4, 12, 26, TLB).

The gift of music provides ample temptation for a believer's pride to get the best of him. Some voices are made for solo parts, others for background. When each voice is committed to harmonize with the others for the edification of the Body, lives are touched by the Spirit. The congregation responds with praise to God. But when a soloist is determined to prove how good he is, or when a background voice decides to demonstrate that he is solo material, look out!

Whenever any gift calls attention to itself, it fails to fulfill God's intention of meeting people's needs. Therefore, whenever you use your gift, ask yourself, "How can I build up the lives of these people? Will my singing, playing, teaching, speaking, or helping benefit them, or just glorify me?"

listen as well as speak

Someone once said, "Maybe God is trying to tell us something by giving us two ears and one mouth." When Paul stood before Felix, the governor, he asked for an expression of kindness. "But, that I may not weary you any further, I beg you to grant us, *by your kindness, a brief hearing*" (Acts 24:4). Paul wanted Felix to listen.

Have you ever talked with someone who wasn't paying attention to you? Your parents? Children? Boss? A friend? Your husband? Your wife? It gets to you, doesn't it? You have something to say. You want to convey an idea. You want to tell someone how you feel. Your listener smiles, nods once in a while, and then changes the conversation. You feel hurt, frustrated, angry.

Now let's reverse the roles for just a minute. A friend has a problem. He desperately wants to share it with you, but he doesn't know how. He gives several hints that he hurts inside. But you turn him off. "We all have problems, Bill. Just pray about it. You know everything will work out fine in the end."

Maybe it's your husband who wants to tell you about his work. Things are rough at the office. His job isn't as secure as it used to be. Younger men are passing him by. He needs someone to talk with, but his pride prevents him from just coming out and saying what's on his mind. Are you listening? Do you make it easy for him to share those thoughts he can barely admit to himself?

Too often we give answers before we hear the problems. The gifted teacher may easily fall into this trap. He may spend hours teaching biblical facts, but never stop to listen to the doubts, hurts, and problems of his students. As Dr. Howard Hendricks puts it, "He scratches where no one itches." Likewise, a counselor may listen just long enough to formulate his opinion about the problem. He quotes some Scripture, has a word of prayer, and opens the door for his client to leave. The counselee walks out frustrated. He never got a chance to share his problem. He vows that he'll never see another counselor. From now on he'll solve his problems by himself or go down trying.

Kindness is different. Kindness says, "You are an important person. You need to share your joys as well as your sorrows. You want to express how you feel. You want to be able to ask questions. Good. I'll listen. I'll be your sounding board. Open your heart."

SPEAK KINDLY

Paul wrote to the Ephesians, "Stop being mean, bad-tempered and angry. Quarreling, harsh words, and dislike of others should have no place in your lives. Instead, *be kind to each other,* tender-hearted, forgiving one another, just as God has forgiven you because you belong to Christ" (Ephesians 4:31, 32, TLB).

According to this context, the opposite of kindness is meanness, anger, quarreling, harshness, and dislike of others. Therefore, we can develop kindness as we first *consider the feelings of those with whom we speak.* Some individuals run roughshod over others. They stereotype people. They speak without the facts. They rush in without caring who gets hurt. They put their minds in neutral and their mouths in high gear. And they leave a trail of broken hearts, crushed wills, and rising tempers.

Don't quarrel. The old adage, "Win an argument, lose a friend," is built on valid observation. Even if you're right, what is gained? During a quarrel we may say something that we'll regret the rest of our lives. The fiercer the argument, the less control we have over our tongues.

It helps to *control the tone and volume with which we speak.* The person who constantly yells or speaks in a rough tone of voice makes few friends. A woman said, "I went up to those people and gave them a piece of my mind. I told them exactly what I thought. And you know, I felt better afterward." Giving people a piece of our mind may make us feel better, but what does it do to them?

There have been times when I've just spoken to my two boys

about something, and they seem to be more zealous to obey than usual. Then my wife asks me, "Why were you so rough with the guys?" I reply, "What do you mean, rough? I just told them to get into their pajamas and get ready for bed." She continues, "I know what you said, but it was how you said it. You sounded like it was a matter of life and death."

"Be kind ... forgiving one another, just as God has forgiven you because you belong to Christ" (Ephesians 4:32, TLB). How has God forgiven you?

He has forgiven you by not holding you accountable for any sin you've ever committed (Colossians 2:13, 14). He has forgiven you by forgetting your sin (Isaiah 43:25). He has forgiven the small things you've done against him, the gross acts you've committed against him and others (1 John 1:9). He has forgiven you as often as you've needed forgiveness (Matthew 18:21, 22).

Is your forgiveness like God's or is it conditional? "I'll forgive this time, but he'd better not try it again!" Or, "He's gone too far this time. I'll remember what he did to me until the day I die. And I'm going to make certain he remembers too!"

Kindness is expressed when you forgive *as* God has forgiven *you.* In other words, forgive as much and as often as the need exists.

ASSOCIATE WITH KIND PEOPLE

Are you aware of the impact that your friends have on you? Peer pressure is more powerful than we imagine. Some of us tell our children, "The kids you run around with are a bad influence on you. Find some other friends." But what about *our* friends? "Oh, they're all Christians!" But to what degree are they living for him? And what is their influence on us?

When I was in school the majority of my friends were also preparing for the ministry, but, more often than I like to remember, we were self-appointed critics. Rather than edify each other, we shared our criticisms.

Often in a church some superspiritual or pseudointellectual group feels "above" everyone else. Much of their time is spent complimenting each other for having "arrived" and criticizing those who haven't. Criticism and sarcasm can spread through a congregation like gangrene, devastating it. Therefore, avoid such people.

In contrast, spend time with those who are excited about Christ, and you'll get excited. Give your time to friends who have a positive outlook on life. You'll see life differently. Remember how Paul influenced other Christians by his positive outlook on adverse circumstances? "Most of the brethren, trusting in the Lord because of my imprisonment, have far more courage to speak the word of God without fear" (Philippians 1:14). The Body of Christ is to operate as a positive influence on its members. "And let us consider how to stimulate one another to love and good deeds, not forsaking our own assembling together, as is the habit of some, but encouraging one another" (Hebrews 10:24, 25).

With whom do you associate? Are you being influenced for good or evil? How do you influence others? You will develop kindness by spending time with those who already demonstrate kindness.

Kindness is part of our new nature. Want to be a man's man? Like a challenge? Dangerous risks? So did Paul. But he made certain that his masculine characteristics included kindness (2 Corinthians 6:4-6).

Do you desire fulfillment as a woman? Would you like your husband and children to praise you? Don't neglect kindness (Proverbs 31:26).

You have the potential to become a very kind person because you have God's Spirit within you. Ask him to develop that unique character trait so that your reputation becomes one of kindness. This is God's will for you. He promises that whatever you ask according to his will, he will grant (1 John 5:14, 15).

pursuing
the good life

What does "the good life" mean to you? Two cars in the garage? A color TV? A good salary? Many associate goodness with life's comforts. Yet, in spite of possessing many of the pleasurable items life offers, many people in our country lack a meaningful life.

When the Bible refers to goodness, it equates the good life with material possessions only when it speaks from man's viewpoint. "But Abraham said, 'Child, remember that during your life you received your good things, and likewise Lazarus bad things; but now he is being comforted here, and you are in agony'" (Luke 16:25).

From God's perspective, however, goodness is a life that is fit, capable, and morally pure. It is a life filled with God, one that demonstrates characteristics of God himself.

ASK how GOD looks at it

No one possesses this kind of goodness on his own. "There is none who does good" (Romans 3:12). At the same time, you and I are expected to possess and experience goodness. "For we are His workmanship, created in Christ Jesus for good works, which God prepared beforehand, that we should walk in them" (Ephesians 2:10).

Sounds like a paradox, doesn't it? We don't have the goodness we need, and yet God holds us responsible to be good. Besides this, you've met many good people who don't even claim to be Christians. Why the confusion? Certainly, some people are good, aren't they?

It depends on where you're standing.

The beautiful San Joaquin Valley in central California experiences sunshine every day during June through August.

It's a filmmaker's paradise. No fears of changing schedule or losing shooting time because of inclement weather. You walk out of the house and remark, "What a beautiful clear day!" And you're right. But a friend says, "You should be here during the winter. Then you can see all the way to the Sierras on the eastern side of the valley." As far as eye can see, the land is flat. You don't take him seriously, but he's right.

Why the problem? Distorted perspective. Valley residents call it "smaze." A mixture of haze from the irrigation in the valley, and summer smog, which, so far, is minimal. Therefore, rather than seeing fifty miles to the horizon, you actually see less than fifty blocks.

The valley looks so clear, the sky so blue. But from a 5,000-foot elevation in the Sierras you witness a brilliant, dark blue sky. In comparison to the mountain view, the sky in the valley is only a light hazy blue.

With similar perspective, we have a certain concept of goodness. We speak of goodness from the standpoint of *skill*. We say, "What a fantastic singer! He's really good." Or in relation to *what satisfies,* we say, "Boy, I've tasted good pies before, but *those* pies are exceptional." Or we see goodness as *external righteousness*. "He's not a Christian, but he's a terrific guy. He doesn't swear, drink, gamble, smoke, use drugs, or indulge in immorality. He's really a good man." We determine goodness by what a person *does*. "Jerry Smith? Yeah. He's a great guy, a family man. His kids are well behaved. They're always doing things together on weekends. No, he doesn't take his family to church, but they go camping a lot. He makes all sorts of sacrifices for others. He's very self-giving. A real good guy."

Each of these examples does demonstrate a type of goodness. But man's view of goodness has its limitations. For instance, it is inferior to God's goodness. God's reply to this standard is revealed by the prophet Isaiah. " 'For My thoughts are not your thoughts, neither are your ways My ways,' declares the Lord. 'For as the heavens are higher than the earth, so are My ways higher

than your ways, and My thoughts than your thoughts' '
55:8, 9). As the view from the mountain is higher and superioi ⌐
the valley view, so God's concept of goodness is higher and
superior to our idea of goodness.

Human standards are flexible and inconsistent. One generation declares, "Adultery is sinful!" The next generation decides
that it's an acceptable way of life as long as both adults consent.
The same can be said about premarital cohabitation, homosexu-
ality, or any other form of immorality. In contrast to man, God's
goodness is inflexible and is consistent with his character. By
nature, God is good. Everything he does, therefore, is good.

The standards given to Moses in the form of commandments
have not changed. The underlying principles of the Law continue
today. God has given man his Law in writing (the ten commandments). And he has given man his Law by means of conscience. Either way, man is held accountable to measure up to
God's standards. "For there is no partiality with God. For all who
have sinned without the Law will also perish without the Law;
and all who have sinned under the Law will be judged by the
Law; for not the hearers of the Law are just before God, but the
doers of the Law will be justified. For when Gentiles who do not
have the Law do instinctively the things of the Law, these, not
having the Law, are a law to themselves, in that they show the
work of the Law written in their hearts, their *conscience* bearing
witness, and their thoughts alternately accusing or else defending
them" (Romans 2:11-15).

That passage provides the reason why a person who never
reads the Bible still walks around with guilt. No one can escape
God's Law and God's judgment. Everyone has a conscience (the
Law of God written into the human heart). The conscience can
be seared, however (1 Timothy 4:2; Ephesians 4:17-19). When
we sin against our conscience time after time, it begins to accept
wrong behavior. We justify our actions. We tell ourselves that
our behavior is right. Eventually we dull the sensitivity of our
conscience. Wrong seems to be right. We treat bad as good.
Guilt is suppressed below the conscious level, and rather than
feel guilty about a specific sin, we live with emptiness.

MEASURING UP TO GOD'S STANDARDS

conscience

When we measure ourselves by God's standard of goodness, we soon recognize there's room for improvement. For instance, do you find it easy to sleep at night, knowing all is well between you and God? If you pass that test, how about your relationship with others? Do you have a clear conscience? The writer to the Hebrews was able to say, "Pray for us, for we are sure that we have a good conscience, desiring to conduct ourselves honorably in all things" (Hebrews 13:18).

reputation

What kind of reputation do you have at work? Industrious? Honest? Ethical? Easy to work with? Cooperative? Or do your fellow workers see you as a person with double standards? One set for the church group and the other for the work crew? How is your reputation at school? An easy pickup? Playboy? Disciplined student? What about at home? An absentee father? An independent-minded wife? A self-willed child? One of the qualifications of a church leader is that he be a man of good reputation (1 Timothy 3:7; Acts 6:3).

fruit

What do our lives produce? The spiritually productive life is the good life. "And those are the ones on whom seed was sown on the *good ground;* and they hear the word, and accept it, and bear fruit, thirty, sixty, and a hundredfold" (Mark 4:20).

The Bible speaks of varying kinds of fruit. The good man will bear fruit by witnessing to the grace of God in his life. "Do you not say, 'There are yet four months, and then comes the harvest'? Behold, I say to you, lift up your eyes, and look on the fields, that they are white for harvest. Already he who reaps is receiving wages, and is *gathering fruit for life eternal*" (John 4:35, 36).

Controlled by God's Holy Spirit, the good person will also produce a Godlike character. "But the fruit of the Spirit is love, joy, peace, patience, kindness, *goodness...*" (Galatians 5:22).

Further, he will experience a fruitful prayer life. He won't be praying in generalities. He won't pray with evil motives. He will speak to God with an expectant heart. The good person will envision the results before they happen. He will know that God is already in the process of answering his prayers. "You did not choose Me, but I chose you, and appointed you, that you should go and bear fruit, and that your fruit should remain, that whatever you ask of the Father in My name, He may give it to you" (John 15:16).

Is your prayer life effective? Or do you approach prayer as some people go to a gambling casino? They put so much on a certain request, just in case they may be lucky and win. A fruitful prayer life isn't a matter of luck. It's a matter of relationship between God and man. "The effective prayer of a righteous man can accomplish much" (James 5:16).

Do you find yourself measuring up to God's standards? Do your conscience, reputation, and spiritual fruit-bearing live up to God's expectations? If you're like the rest of us, there's probably room for improvement.

GETTING AND KEEPING IN SPIRITUAL CONDITION

A few years ago I decided to take karate lessons. My basic motive was curiosity. I never intended to use that skill except in an emergency, and then I'd probably look for another way out.

I had to overcome two barriers. The first barrier was deciding actually to take the instruction. I had wanted karate instruction ten years earlier, but I never made the decision to sign up. I only thought about it.

Once that barrier was overcome, I now faced a second problem. I had to keep in condition by spending the first half hour or more of each lesson going through grueling exercises. The motto was, "If it doesn't hurt, you're not working hard enough."

I decided to commit myself to both objectives. And, until my instructor broke two of my ribs, I learned far more than I expected. I also found myself in the best physical condition since high school.

Spiritual conditioning faces two comparable barriers. First there is the initial decision of commitment to Jesus Christ. Then there is the daily problem of keeping spiritually fit.

COMMITMENT GETS YOU STARTED

One day as Jesus spoke to the Pharisees he said, "Either make the tree good, and its fruit good; or make the tree rotten, and its fruit rotten; for the tree is known by its fruit" (Matthew 12:33).

Some people attempt to produce a good life out of an evil heart, and it comes across phony. The Pharisees were religious leaders. They displayed all the religious acts of righteousness, but inwardly they were corrupt. Jesus denounced their hypocrisy. "They do all their deeds to be noticed by men ... they love the place of honor at banquets" (Matthew 23:5, 6).

Perhaps you're trying to be like Christ. You try to love others, but fail. You want to be patient, but you blow it every time. You promise yourself that you'll be different, but you stay the same.

If you acknowledge your own inability to be the Christlike individual you should be, God will honor that attitude. But you must begin by committing yourself to him. Open your inner self to Jesus Christ. Invite him to enter your life and change the real you from the inside out. Pray something like this:

"Lord, I have no goodness of my own to offer. According to your standards, I don't measure up. I'll never make it. So I ask you to forgive me. I ask you to enter my life right now. Make me the person you want me to be. Give me your goodness and righteousness. Thank you for answering my prayer. In Jesus' name, Amen."

If you have just now prayed this prayer with a sincere heart, Jesus has entered your life. You possess his goodness. But in order to experience that goodness in daily living, some basic spiritual exercises must become part of your life.

SPIRITUAL EXERCISE KEEPS YOU FIT

At the outset of this chapter I described goodness as a life that is fit, capable, and morally pure. Spiritual fitness can be maintained by continuous exercise. Here are four essential exercises for spiritual conditioning.

begin with scriptural saturation

Get into the Word as regularly as possible. Don't make a fetish out of Bible reading. But study the Word, allowing it to filter through your heart, mind, and will. The psalmist declared, "How can a young man keep his way pure? By keeping it according to Thy word" (Psalm 119:9). The New Testament teaches, "All Scripture is inspired by God and profitable for teaching, for reproof, for correction, for training in righteousness; that the man of God may be adequate, equipped for every good work" (2 Timothy 3:16, 17). Good works are the result of a life trained in righteousness.

exercise your prayer life

Too many Christians have gotten into the habit of using God as a fire escape. They handle life according to their own desires until they get into deep trouble. Then they cry out to God for help. But there's a better way.

When you approach God as Father, an entirely different attitude emerges. It's not so much one of a creature calling to his Creator for help, but rather a child speaking to his heavenly Parent. When I relate to God as my Father, I want to thank him for his provisions. I get excited about his guidance in my life. I'm not surprised when he meets my needs because I'm his child. And if I need food, he won't give me a stone (Matthew 7:9). Praying and praising are intermixed as I talk with my Father. I don't have to bargain with him. I don't have to plead. He knows my needs, feelings, and attitudes, and he provides accordingly. To bring him my burdens and perplexities, joys and praises, is as common as breathing. Why? Because God is not only my Lord. He is my Father.

rely upon Christ daily to live his life through you

He said, "I am the vine, you are the branches; he who abides in Me, and I in him, he bears much fruit; for apart from Me you can do nothing" (John 15:5).

Of course human beings perform all types of deeds outside of Jesus Christ. This isn't what the Lord means. He is referring to spiritual performance. The believer accomplishes no spiritually significant work outside of reliance upon Jesus.

Jesus gives spiritual wisdom for proper action. He provides power to overcome temptation. He opens doors for spiritual service. Jesus declared that we are spiritually helpless without him; Paul proclaimed, "I can do all things through Him who strengthens me" (Philippians 4:13).

How easy it is to rely on a certain method, a special gift, a former experience, an outstanding personality, a brilliant mind, or an earned degree. As we use these provisions of God we see him bless. And then we reason, "It must be my personality, looks, or gift that is making such an impact on people."

About this time the Lord lovingly reminds us that such tools don't produce the results any more than a hammer drives a nail on its own. God may lead us through a humiliating experience so that we see ourselves as we are—helpless without him. He may choose a painful circumstance that causes us to cry to him. The Lord may use an overpowering situation to help us see that unless he takes over, we've had it.

This is all part of the Father's pruning work. "And every branch that bears fruit, He prunes it, that it may bear more fruit" (John 15:2). God's desire is not to hurt us. He does not attempt to get even. Nor does he want us to be miserable. God's purpose is both to prevent and correct self-reliance. The only way we can bear spiritual fruit is by depending upon Jesus rather than ourselves.

confess personal sin

This sin may take the form of pride, jealousy, bitterness, immorality, drunkenness, an uncontrolled tongue, gluttony, or self-reliance. As the Holy Spirit brings conviction into your heart, deal with the sin immediately. Otherwise you'll spend hours, days, even weeks, in defeat and guilt. As you confess and as God cleanses, you are again prepared to experience the good life. "Therefore, if a man cleanses himself from these things, he will be a vessel for honor, sanctified, useful to the Master, prepared for every good work" (2 Timothy 2:21).

INTEGRATING GOODNESS WITH GIFTS

Barnabas is called a good man (Acts 11:24). He exhibited God's goodness by using the gift of exhortation, especially encouraging young believers in the faith (Acts 11:22-24)

Another example of goodness integrated with a spiritual gift is the life of Dorcas, a woman who was a gifted craftsperson. She made a tremendous impact on other women in Joppa by her gifts of craftsmanship and mercy along with her good character. Luke provided a small glimpse of her life. The occasion: Dorcas' funeral. "As soon as he [Peter] arrived, they took him upstairs where Dorcas lay. The room was filled with weeping widows who were showing one another the coats and other garments Dorcas had made for them." Earlier, Luke described this woman's character: "a believer who was always doing kind things for others, especially the poor" (Acts 9:36, 39, TLB).

What spiritual gift do you possess? Showing mercy? Helping? Teaching? Music? When your gift is integrated with a character that is fit, capable, and morally pure, you will experience a fullness of joy. God will bless your service. The good life will no longer be a materialistic dream; it will become a spiritual reality.

you can count on it

The late Dr. V. Raymond Edman of Wheaton College often said to his students, "It's always too soon to quit." The Apostle Paul expressed the same idea when he wrote, "And let us not lose heart in doing good, for in due time we shall reap if we do not grow weary" (Galatians 6:9).

Quitting is a trap. The college student asks, "What am I going to do with my life?" A year passes and he hasn't found the answer. A second year passes and the answer still evades him. He becomes frustrated and drops out of school to travel another route.

Jim is another quitter, though his approach is different. He volunteers for a church office. He agrees to take a Sunday school class. He tells the superintendent, "If you ever need any help, don't hesitate to call." But where is Jim when he's needed? Who doesn't show up at the meetings? Who comes ill-prepared to class every Sunday? Jim doesn't quit his position. He just keeps a more responsible person from getting it.

The Scriptures describe this irritating habit without equivocation, "Like a bad tooth and an unsteady foot is confidence in a faithless man in time of trouble" (Proverbs 25:19). An undependable Christian is one who hasn't allowed the Holy Spirit to develop in him the fruit of faithfulness (Galatians 5:22).

TAKE YOUR MEASUREMENTS

Jesus told a parable about faithful and unfaithful servants. From this story we can learn how faithfulness is measured.

There are those who excuse their lack of follow-through on the basis of possessing few gifts. "I'm not very gifted. I can't sing or teach. If I only possessed the gifts Janet has, I'd really be dependable."

But in Jesus' parable, the man who had two talents was just as faithful as the one who was given five talents (a talent was worth $1,000 in silver). The master expected the one-talented man to be as faithful as the other two servants.

Another Christian comes to the conclusion, "My results are never as great as John's. There's no way to compete with him and come out on top. I'm quitting!"

Again, the master in the parable didn't put one servant in competition with another. He expected each to give a return on what he had. The two-talented man wasn't expected to produce five talents. But he was capable of making two more talents. The master called him "faithful" (Matthew 25:23).

Faithfulness isn't measured by how much we have, nor is it measured by the abundance of results. *Faithfulness is measured by what we do with what God has given us.*

faithfulness looks for a place to "happen"

Faithfulness should begin with the total *life style*. If I know Jesus personally, my life should reflect that experience. The Bible describes spiritual conversion as coming from darkness into light (1 Peter 2:9). It speaks about a transfer out of death and into life (John 5:24). Paul wrote, "Therefore if any man is in Christ, he is a new creature; the old things passed away; behold, new things have come" (2 Corinthians 5:17).

How's my language? Full of criticism? Do dirty jokes keep passing from my lips? Or the old four-letter words when people irritate me?

Let's check attitudes. Am I holding a grudge? Nursing that old bitterness toward my former friend? Jealous because someone else got "my" promotion?

Any old habits I need to forsake? Has my family pleaded with me to give up certain habits? Is the Holy Spirit bringing conviction into my life? The Apostle Paul declared, "All things are lawful for me, but not all things are profitable. All things are lawful for me, but I will not be mastered by anything" (1 Corinthians 6:12). The habits of overeating, overwork, laziness, or any other carryover from the old life must be placed at Jesus' feet.

Faithfulness should also make its way into my *service for Christ.* So many good projects have been started and later abandoned because some Christian was undependable. The Lord's work cannot operate on good intentions. Jesus said, "No one, after putting his hand to the plow and looking back, is fit for the kingdom of God" (Luke 9:62).

When the Lord challenged his followers about the cost of discipleship he said, "For which one of you, when he wants to build a tower, does not first sit down and calculate the cost, to see if he has enough to complete it? Otherwise, when he has laid a foundation and is not able to finish, all who observe it begin to ridicule him, saying, 'This man began to build and was not able to finish' " (Luke 14:28-30). Any unfinished projects? Let me encourage you to complete what you've started. Maybe it won't turn out as you wanted. Perhaps you'll have to settle for limited objectives. But finish it anyway.

We should aim to be faithful in *managing our affairs* (time, spiritual gifts, money, family).

How often have you replied to a request, "I'd love to help, but I just don't have the time"? What about those situations where you promised yourself you'd get to it, but time escaped you? You never got to it. Well, welcome to the human race! We are fellow procrastinators.

Time management. The Scriptures tell us to "redeem the time," that is, use every moment effectively (Ephesians 5:16). This means I should have enough time for God, for my family, for myself, and for others.

There are ways to improve our time management. We can first evaluate how we are using time. For instance, as Moses led Israel through the wilderness, he felt he needed more than a twenty-four-hour day to accomplish his tasks (Exodus 18:17, 18). He and the people were wearing down. His problem? Moses spent too much time with the urgent (counseling, vv. 14-16) and not enough time with the necessary (teaching, vv. 19, 20; delegating, vv. 21, 22).

Then, organize your time. Write down what is important to you. As a housewife it's important for you to take care of your children, clean house, grocery shop, prepare meals, study the Bible for yourself, pray, etc. Now rearrange that list by determining what is really important (don't confuse the urgent with the important). You may want to use numbers (#1, #2, #3) to assign your priorities.

Follow your schedule. Complete task #1 before you move on to project #2. It's easy to get bogged down at this point. But here's where prayer becomes effective. When you don't feel like doing task #2, ask God for the discipline to do it anyway, and then move on to complete the job.

Managing our spiritual gifts. Peter informed his readers, "As each one has received a special gift, employ it in serving one another, as good stewards [managers] of the manifold grace of God" (1 Peter 4:10). Your spiritual gift is a stewardship, a responsibility to be managed effectively.

Peter provided two principles for managing gifts properly. We must first employ our gifts. Someone has said, "The man who does not read is no better off than the man who cannot read." Likewise, a man who does not use his spiritual gift is no better off than a man who does not have that spiritual gift. The gift must be put to work.

A second principle Peter presented focuses on the purpose of gifts. These gifts are to be used to serve others. Too often our gifts serve only ourselves and our immediate family.

Money management is another area in which to be faithful. Jesus said, "And if you are untrustworthy about worldly wealth, who will trust you with the true riches of heaven? And if you are not faithful with other people's money, why should you be entrusted with money of your own ... you cannot serve both God and money" (Luke 16:11-13, TLB). We serve money when we allow it to control us.

If we were to analyze our buying habits we would probably

admit that we were allowing the world system to pour us into its mold (Romans 12:2, Phillips). At times we buy because we're told that the new product is better than the old. The old may be very functional, but because of some additional gadget or change of style, we replace the old with the new. We also buy because some object has broken. Rather than fix it, we convince ourselves we need a new one. Sometimes we do; more often we don't.

Then there are those sales. "It must be God's will. It was a good deal!" Actually, it's only a good deal if you really need the item.

Sometimes we buy because the terms are easy. "Buy it today," we're told. "The first payment won't be due for two months. Use your Master Charge or Bankamericard." Living today on tomorrow's money can prove dangerous. The Bible warns, "Instruct those who are rich in this present world not to be conceited or to fix their hope on *the uncertainty of riches,* but on God, who richly supplies us with all things to enjoy" (1 Timothy 6:17). Overuse of credit buying brings the experience Israel had many years ago, "You plant much but harvest little. You have scarcely enough to eat or drink, and not enough clothes to keep you warm. Your income disappears, as though you were putting it into pockets filled with holes" (Haggai 1:6, TLB).

Another poor reason for buying is just because we want something. A desire for an object in itself isn't wrong. But if we must rob God for it, then we sin against him. If we go into great debt "just because we want it," our judgment has become dulled.

The Bible is emphatic about controlling natural appetites. "Like an athlete I punish my body, treating it roughly, training it to do what it should, not what it wants to" (1 Corinthians 9:27, TLB).

Perhaps the poorest excuse for buying is because someone else has one. A wife nags her husband, "But honey, Bob and Sally just bought new furniture, and they don't make as much as we do. Do you want them to think that you aren't a good provider?" Or a husband tells his wife, "Look, everybody in the car pool has a new stereo. I feel left out when the guys talk about their new equipment."

There is nothing necessarily wrong with having a new car, a roomful of furniture, or a stereo set. The two extremes to avoid are (1) guilt because we have something new or nice and (2) covetousness (always grasping for something more).

Here are a few questions that may help as you decide about buying.

Will I honor the Lord if I buy it?

Will I use it for the benefit of others?

Will it help or hinder my reputation for Christ?

Will it help meet needs?

Will it advance the Lord's work?

Will I enjoy it as much in another month?

Am I willing to wait until I can afford it?

Managing our families. Besides being managers of our time, spiritual gifts, and money, we are to manage the affairs of our family. The Bible tells us that children are a gift of the Lord (Psalm 127:3). Proper family management is a prerequisite for church leadership. "He must be one who manages his own household well, keeping his children under control with all dignity (but if a man does not know how to manage his own household, how will he take care of the children of God?)" (1 Timothy 3:4, 5).

God holds us fathers responsible to be faithful in teaching and disciplining our children. "Fathers, don't scold your children so much that they become discouraged and quit trying" (Colossians 3:21, TLB). A father who places too much responsibility upon his children's shoulders and expects perfection will frustrate and discourage them. A father who allows his children to do whatever they please will soon be in trouble. "Rather, bring them up with the loving discipline the Lord himself approves, with suggestions and godly advice" (Ephesians 6:4b, TLB).

HOW TO BECOME MORE FAITHFUL

Three basic questions are helpful as we search for practical ways to develop faithfulness.

What does God expect of me?

What are my resources?
For what am I accountable?

what's my line?

A steward is a manager. He manages the affairs of another. Since God's affairs cover the entire universe, how are we to discern our particular responsibility? One way is to make a checklist of what God has already revealed to us.

Check the Biblical imperatives (commands). Wherever a direct command appears for the believer, accept this as part of your responsibility. Jesus said, "A new commandment I give to you, that you love one another, even as I have loved you, that you also love one another" (John 13:34). How are you performing in this area? Husband, do you show love to your wife as Christ showed his love for the church (Ephesians 5:25)? Wife, do you love your husband and children to the extent that you will submit to him and spend time with them (Titus 2:4, 5)? How about that individual with whom you've just argued, that person who is constantly provoking you, the guy who is determined to get even with you? Do you love them (Matthew 5:44-48)?

Another imperative focuses on maintaining spiritual unity in the church (Ephesians 4:1-3; 1 Corinthians 12:25; Philippians 2:1, 2). How well do you work with others? Is your service for the Lord one of competition or cooperation?

Another imperative appeals to the control center of life. Paul exhorts us to "be filled with the Holy Spirit" (Ephesians 5:18). A better rendering of this verse would be, "Keep on being filled with the Holy Spirit." The control of the Spirit over my life is not a "once for all" event. It must become a daily experience. Who is in control of your life right now? If you're filled with bitterness, self-pity, anger, lust, or unbelief, then it's not the Holy Spirit. But if you sense an attitude of love, understanding, a meek and gentle spirit, then thank God that he is still in control.

There are hundreds of imperatives throughout Scripture, which God expects us to be faithful in fulfilling in his strength. But beyond the commands we can narrow our responsibility by *considering our spiritual gifts.* What is yours? If God has given you the gift of teaching, but you don't teach, what good is that? If you have the gift of music but you refuse to be involved musically, who is being helped? If your gift is giving, but you don't give, your unfaithfulness hinders the progress of God's work.

On the other hand, you aren't responsible to do what God has not equipped you to do. (By this I don't mean that you should refuse to help out in an emergency just because that's not your gift. But then you need not serve with a guilt complex because you're not highly qualified.) Discover your gift, and seek a ministry where you can faithfully use it (Romans 12:6-8; 1 Peter 4:10).

Check the needs that exist. Am I qualified to meet any of those needs?

When God led Philip the evangelist to Samaria, he expected Philip to preach Christ to a people who had not heard. Multitudes of Samaritans heard and responded to the good news of salvation (Acts 8:5, 6, 12). Then another need arose. These new believers knew nothing about the Holy Spirit.[1] So the Jerusalem church sent Peter and John to visit the new congregation in Samaria. When they arrived, they laid their hands on the new believers so that the Holy Spirit would enter their lives. Then, since they were gifted prophets, Peter and John expounded the Scriptures in greater depth than Philip had. Once the Samaritans began their growth process, Peter and John left the area.

A similar illustration of changing needs is given in Acts 11. The city of Antioch was first invaded by lay witnesses, evangelizing for Christ (vv. 19-21). Then came Barnabas who had the gift of exhortation. He was able to encourage the new Christians as well as lead others to Christ (vv. 22-24). The need arose for sound teaching of the Word, so Barnabas sent for Saul (Paul), a gifted teacher. Another need became known when some prophets came down to Antioch from Jerusalem saying that a famine was going to hit the land. This would mean a hardship on

[1]Today you and I receive the Holy Spirit *at the same time* that we receive Jesus Christ as Savior (Ephesians 1:13; Romans 8:9). But during the transition period in the early church, when the gospel was proclaimed to a new group, the Holy Spirit was given at different times (at salvation to the Jews—Acts 2:38-42; after salvation to the Samaritans [half Jew-half gentile]—Acts 8:12, 15-17; at salvation to the Gentiles—Acts 10:44-48; after salvation to the disciples of John the Baptist—Acts 19:1-7).

Christians, especially in Judea, where many had lost their jobs because of their faith in Christ. In this way the church at Antioch was challenged to supply the physical needs of the believers in Judea (Acts 11:29).

Check the leading of the Holy Spirit. What is the Spirit of God specifically leading you to do? Perhaps you don't know. I assure you that you can know. The Spirit made his directives known to the church in Antioch for Paul and Barnabas. He gave further direction to Paul and his companions when he led them to Macedonia (Acts 16:6-10). He may lead you through the encouragement of a friend. He may choose some circumstance that has obviously been arranged by God. You may sense the still, small voice within, prompting you to a specific decision.

God doesn't play hide and seek. He wants you to know. James writes, "You do not have because you do not ask" (James 4:2). Why not put this book down right now and tell God, "Lord, I want anything and everything you want for me. I desire to do your will, whatever it is. I give you the right to show me as much or as little as you desire. Just lead me today in the way I should go." If you've sincerely sought the Lord for his guidance, expect him to reply. It may not be as you'd planned, but you won't be disappointed. The Holy Spirit loves to lead available people to streams of refreshing water.

what do I have to work with?

As you begin to discover what God wants you to accomplish, you'd better check your resources. Jesus warned, "For which one of you, when he wants to build a tower, does not first sit down and calculate the cost, to see if he has enough to complete it?" (Luke 14:28).

Will I be able to do the job? Will God ask me to do something for which I'm not qualified? Relax. God will never lead you to any task that is too great for him to accomplish through you.

You see, the abiding presence of Jesus Christ is in you, if you've extended that invitation to him (Revelation 3:20). On one of the many occasions when the Apostle Paul faced a tense situation, Jesus appeared to him saying, "Do not be afraid any longer, but go on speaking and do not be silent; for I am with you, and no man will attack you in order to harm you, for I have many people in this city" (Acts 18:9, 10).

Do you have a team concept when you serve the Lord? Jesus is your partner. When you're ready to throw in the towel, you can tell him, "Lord, you'll have to take it from here. I just can't do it!" Paul's testimony is, "For I can do everything God asks me to with the help of Christ who gives me the strength and power" (Philippians 4:13, TLB).

The power of the Holy Spirit is available to you. As you seek the Spirit's power to be released in your life, you will experience faithfulness in your witnessing (Acts 1:8; 1 Corinthians 2:4), faithfulness in expecting great things from God (Romans 15:13; Ephesians 3:20, 21), and faithfulness in suffering (2 Timothy 1:8). If it were up to us, we would "fold" under the pressures of everyday life. But by God's power, we can become faithful stewards of all God entrusts into our hands.

Besides the presence of Jesus Christ and the power of the Holy Spirit, God has given each of us the mind of Christ (1 Corinthians 2:16; John 15:15), the gifts of the Spirit (1 Corinthians 12:4, 7-11), the character of the Spirit (Galatians 5:22, 23), and the Body of Christ (1 Corinthians 12:21, 25).

God has never told us to be loners. He does not give us assignments and then abandon us. He gives us responsibility and ability, and then he blesses us so that we can faithfully achieve his goals.

the winner's circle

The way so many Christians live, you'd think that God rejoices in losers. Some individuals believe that mediocrity is spiritual. But the Scriptures indicate the opposite. "And let us not get tired of doing what is right, for after a while we will reap a harvest of blessing if we don't get discouraged and give up" (Galatians 6:9, TLB). "And in whatever he does, he prospers" (Psalm 1:3).

The faithful steward (manager) cannot lose. His blessings may seem delayed. His patience may be tested. But God won't allow faithfulness to go unrewarded.

dove power

The bear symbolizes the Soviet Union. The lion depicts England; the eagle, the United States. Each represents pride and power.

Advertisers can't sell perfume *per se* to men, so they label it "Hai Karate." Now you can be a he-man and smell good at the same time. Automobile manufacturers know that the public would reject a car branded "Donkey," "Kitty Cat," "Minnow," "Sparrow," "Turtle," or "Gartersnake." Even though a name doesn't help the car to perform any better, people will buy a name: Mustang, Cougar, Barracuda, Thunderbird, Stingray, or Cobra. All these names depict strength.

BUT I DON'T WANT TO BE MEEK!

meekness is not weakness

When Jesus, the Lord of the universe, came to earth he arrived as a helpless, dependent infant. He was called the Lamb of God. He was meek and lowly, "gentle and humble in heart" (Matthew 11:29). Jesus shows us that it is possible to be gentle and yet strong. The individual who refuses to be meek usually doesn't understand what meekness means.

meekness is not refusing to take a stand

The meek or gentle person is often accused of being an introvert or man pleaser. William Blake, an eighteenth-century English poet, referred to Jesus as "meek and mild." Jesus' disciple Matthew wrote, "And Jesus entered the temple and cast out all those who were buying and selling in the temple, and overturned the tables of the moneychangers and the seats of those who were selling doves" (Matthew 21:12).

Later in his Gospel, Matthew described a conversation Jesus had with the religious leaders: "Woe to you, scribes and Pharisees, hypocrites ... Woe to you, blind guides ... you fools and blind men ... you serpents, you brood of vipers, how shall you escape the sentence of hell?" (Matthew 23:13-33). That doesn't sound like a weak, wishy-washy person. It took a man to stand against the leaders of the day. Yes, Jesus was gentle and meek, but he was also strong and filled with convictions which he defended.

meekness is not an exclusively feminine characteristic

The Bible insists that meekness is characteristic of the Holy Spirit (Galatians 5:23—"gentleness") and is to be representative of church leadership (1 Timothy 3:2, 3).

meekness is not incompatible with exercising discipline

"And the Lord's bond-servant must not be quarrelsome, but be kind to all, able to teach, patient when wronged, *with gentleness correcting* those who are in opposition" (2 Timothy 2:24, 25). Discipline does not mean threatening and beating. Discipline does not mean losing my temper and yelling at the top of my lungs. To discipline is to train. Sometimes we use preventive discipline to protect our children and friends from trouble. At other times we may have to use corrective discipline. But when we do, we should be gentle. This was the instruction Paul gave to

Pastor Timothy, "Do not sharply rebuke an older man, but rather appeal to him as a father, to the younger men as brothers, the older women as mothers, and the younger women as sisters, in all purity" (1 Timothy 5:1, 2).

WHAT IS GENTLENESS?

gentleness expresses itself in cooperation

The individual who insists that his ideas and opinions be accepted is not gentle. Church leaders in particular are "to be uncontentious, gentle, showing every consideration for all men" (Titus 3:2). This doesn't mean that we agree with every opinion, nor does it mean that strong support for an opinion is unspiritual. But gentleness does imply that we cooperate with one another. We show respect for one another. We listen to what each has to say. Then we evaluate and attempt to come to a mutual decision on the issue at hand. Paul expressed the same idea in another way: "with all humility and gentleness, with patience, showing forbearance to one another in love, being diligent to preserve the unity of the Spirit in the bond of peace" (Ephesians 4:2, 3).

gentleness expresses itself in humility

But what is that? Many think it's an attitude of self-debasement. "I am nothing. I'm a nobody. I have no gifts. Nothing to contribute. Poor me!" That is not humility.

Humility is an attitude that accepts myself as God made me. It recognizes my strengths and weaknesses. Humility knows that "every good and perfect gift comes from above." It thanks God for all he has provided to make life worth living.

Humility and gentleness go together in the book of Galatians. "Brethren, even if a man is caught in any trespass, you who are spiritual, restore such a one in a spirit of gentleness; looking to yourselves, lest you too be tempted ... For if anyone thinks he is something when he is nothing, he deceives himself" (Galatians 6:1, 3).

When is a man nothing? When he attempts to overcome temptation in his own strength. When he thinks he is above the sin of the one he is restoring to fellowship. None of us is a match for the wiles and devices of Satan. We should be aware that "the heart is more deceitful than all else and is desperately sick" (Jeremiah 17:9). A humble person maintains an accurate self-image and therefore can be gentle with others.

gentleness expresses itself in teachability

The know-it-all is not gentle because he is unteachable. He refuses to listen and learn, and so he remains stupid and cocky. But the gentle person is a learner. James writes, "Therefore putting aside all filthiness and all that remains of wickedness, in humility [gentleness] receive the word implanted, which is able to save your souls" (James 1:21).

Jesus Christ was a teacher, but he was also a learner. "Although He was a Son, He learned obedience from the things which He suffered" (Hebrews 5:8). This passage does not imply that Jesus was ever disobedient. One can learn obedience without being disobedient. If I learn the rules of a new game, I am learning to be obedient to the rules. I can learn by breaking them and paying the consequences or I can learn by understanding what they are and immediately submitting to them.

Jesus was obedient to his Father's will to the point of death (Philippians 2:8). He always did what pleased his Father. The best learners often make the best teachers. And it is Jesus the Teacher who appeals, "Take My yoke upon you, and learn from me, for I am gentle and humble in heart, and you shall find rest for your souls. For My yoke is easy, and my load is light" (Matthew 11:29, 30).

gentleness expresses itself in submission

"In the same way, you wives, be submissive to your own husbands ... with the imperishable quality of a gentle and quiet spirit" (1 Peter 3:1, 4). Many a woman wants to remake her husband. She determines to set him straight. She may develop a nagging or whining or manipulative spirit. The more she pushes, the greater his resistance.

A wife has the right to be loved, noticed, and complimented by her husband. But when she demands his attention and threatens him by withholding sexual relations or tells him to cook his own meals, she is cooking her goose. Few men respond positively to a woman's threats or demands. But they will respond to a gentle and quiet spirit, demonstrated by a submissive will.

DEVELOP GENTLENESS

Some Christians have a difficult time understanding that they have the potential to be gentle. Perhaps because of past experiences they feel they must be tough. They think that unless they are aggressive everyone is going to walk all over them. But when the Holy Spirit comes into our lives he brings with him the quality of gentleness. So, how can we allow the Holy Spirit to develop gentleness in us as individuals?

LOOK AT MOTHERS

Consider a motherlike love. Paul writes, "But we proved to be gentle among you, as a nursing mother tenderly cares for her own children. Having thus a fond affection for you, we were well pleased to impart to you not only the gospel of God but also our own lives, because you had become very dear to us. For you recall, brethren, our labor and hardship, how working night and day so as not to be a burden to any of you, we proclaimed to you the gospel of God" (1 Thessalonians 2:7-9).

A nursing mother is tender with her child. She holds the child to her breast, strokes the child's head, touches his nose, and allows him to grab her fingers. She isn't harsh, complaining, or demanding. She wants to satisfy the need of her child.

As a nursing mother feeds her child, a gentle person is one who nourishes and edifies other Christians. The Bible describes various ways in which we can do this.

We can share the Word with one another. Perhaps God has impressed you with some truth that someone else needs to hear. As you share it, another will be edified [built up] (Acts 20:32). Showing people how much we know may be a big ego boost to us, but loving them will enable them to be edified. Paul said, "Knowledge makes arrogant, but love edifies" (1 Corinthians 8:1).

Visit a friend when she is distressed, and your display of love will be an encouragement. Listen as she pours her heart out to you. Your response can also be edifying. "Let no unwholesome word proceed from your mouth, but only such a word as is good for edification according to the need of the moment, that it may give grace to those who hear" (Ephesians 4:29). A word of encouragement when we're ready to throw in the towel is like a breath of fresh air. The adrenalin begins to flow again. Our vision is renewed. We're prepared to tackle our problems once more.

Remember also the sacrifices a nursing mother must make. She is willing to pay the price for the good of her child: a two A.M. feeding, a five A.M. feeding. The little alarm that goes off in the baby's stomach is heard throughout the house. Mother rises to meet the need. Like a nursing mother, the Apostle Paul served others by "working night and day" (1 Thessalonians 2:9; Acts 18:1-3).

LOOK AT FATHERS

"Just as you know how we were exhorting and encouraging and imploring each one of you as a father would his own children, so that you may walk in a manner worthy of the God who calls you into His own kingdom and glory" (1 Thessalonians 2:11, 12).

In this passage the Apostle Paul was speaking of preventive discipline. (The writer to the Hebrews spoke of corrective discipline—Hebrews 12:4-13.) Note the three words Paul used to describe how a father trains his children.

He *exhorts* them. The word translated "exhorting" means to call to one's side. Here is a father sitting down with his son or daughter by his side, having a heart-to-heart talk. I feel closest to my own boys when I sit on the edge of their beds at night.

Sometimes one of them will say, "Dad, tell me what it was like when you were my age." Or, "Some of the kids at school were swearing and they tried to get me to go along with them. I was really tempted, but I didn't do it." What a time to share the fact that dads also have temptations!

A father also disciplines by *encouraging* (cheering up, comforting). Your son loses his baseball game. Your daughter wasn't asked to go to some school function. Cheer them up. Comfort them. Encourage them to go on with the Lord (Hebrews 3:13; 10:25).

A third approach to preventive discipline is *imploring*. The word "implore" originally meant to "declare" or "testify." Paul used the term in the sense of warning. Discussing the moral aspects of our sexual lives he wrote, "For this is the will of God, your sanctification; that is, that you abstain from sexual immorality ... and that no man transgress and defraud his brother in the matter because the Lord is the avenger in all these things, just as we also told you before and *solemnly warned* you" (1 Thessalonians 4:3, 6).

The book of Proverbs contains hundreds of verses given by a father to his son (Proverbs 1:8, 10; 2:1; 3:1, 11; 4:1, 10, 20; 5:1, 7; 6:1, 20; 7:1, etc.) The father warns his son about foolishness, prostitutes, mismanagement of money, control of the tongue, "get rich quick" schemes, etc.

When we watch some friend getting himself into difficulty, we should refuse to take the attitude, "Well, it's his life. I'm not going to interfere." Imploring him from a heart of love with a tender spirit is not interference. If our friend refuses to heed the warning, then we must place him in the Lord's hands. But the least we can do is to warn him of the consequences and plead with him to turn from his foolishness.

"UNLESS YOU BECOME AS A LITTLE CHILD"

A third approach to gentleness is childlike dependency. I'm not implying that as adults we should become leeches on society, but that we should recognize our dependence on God and the Body of Christ.

Too often we're afraid to admit we have needs. Seldom does a husband come to me and say, "Pastor, we've got problems." Ninety-five percent of my marriage counseling begins with the wife. The husband sits at home grumbling, "What problems? We don't have any problems!"

Often church leaders can't admit that they have problems. "I'm supposed to be a spiritual leader in my church. People would lose respect for me if they knew..."

When we refuse to admit we have problems we remove the opportunity for someone to use his gentleness to help us. It's like the hand saying to the foot, "I have no need of you." All members of the Body are necessary. If we never admit any need, we miss some of the greatest personal relationships two people can have: loving and being loved; caring and being cared for.

Hardly a Wednesday evening passes that I don't tell my people, "Please pray for me this week. I'm having difficulty with my message for Sunday. I don't know what God has in store for us, but I'd appreciate your prayer support." I've found not only a closer relationship with my people, but a greater insight into the Scriptures because they brought me before God.

But how does dependency help me to become more gentle? I become more gentle as I depend on a gentle God to use any means he desires to fill my inadequacies. I begin to know that I don't know. I come to realize the limitations of my abilities. At the same time I experience his sufficiency. "Not that we are adequate in ourselves to consider anything coming from ourselves, but our adequacy is from God" (2 Corinthians 3:5).

Then, when I work with others and notice their flaws, quirks, and inadequacies, I need not be brash and cruel or make unreasonable demands. They are as inadequate without God as I. With an understanding heart, I can respond to them with gentleness.

HIGHLY QUALIFIED TO BE UTTERLY USELESS

I'll never forget hearing Dr. Howard Hendricks speak about Moses. He described the first forty years of his life as being "highly qualified to be utterly useless." Moses had the education, prestige, and power to be a great leader, but something was lacking: a personal relationship with God.

So the Lord arranged for Moses to spend the next forty years leading sheep. During this time, away from the life and influence of Egypt, Moses began his "liberal arts education." He took such courses as *Wilderness Survival 101*. Then there was *Shepherding 101* which included how to find, protect, lead, shear, and be patient with straying sheep. He also enrolled in a required course known as *Basic Theology 101*. This was the toughy. He had to begin with the name of God: "Then Moses said to God, 'Behold, I am going to the sons of Israel, and I shall say to them, The God of your fathers has sent me to you. Now they may say to me, What is His name? What shall I say to them?' " (Exodus 3:13). Moses didn't even know God's name. As time passed he came to know a lot about God.

Along with his theology course, Moses took *Anthropology 101*. He learned about human nature. He learned that a brother and sister can get you into a lot of difficulty. He learned that those you think are your closest friends can turn against you. He learned that without God, his ability to function properly was zilch (Numbers 11:14, 15).

If you were to categorize the life of Moses with one word what would you choose? Leader? Statesman? Law-giver? The Bible has chosen an interesting term for this leader of Israel, this man's man. The quality is given in Numbers 12:3. "Now the man Moses was *very humble*, more than any man who was on the face of the earth." What a way to describe this great man! In spite of his anger with his people, in spite of the times he had to warn and rebuke, Moses was a *gentle man*.

A strong-willed individualist may think he is God's gift to mankind, but in God's sight he is useless. He exaggerates his strengths and underestimates his weaknesses. The world may admire him, but God resists the proud and gives grace to the humble. Eventually he brings down the proud and exalts the humble.

If you are a born-again child of God, the potential for gentleness lies within you. Humble yourself before God and he will exalt you at the proper time (1 Peter 5:6).

learning to say no

The compulsive eater, the spendthrift, the student who seldom studies, the Christian who lacks a devotional life, and the immoral person all lack one basic essential: *self-control.*

Most people, in fact, lack self-control in some area of life. One individual may be a disciplined student, but maintain poor eating habits. Another may manage his time well, but mismanage his money.

Without self-discipline, hopes remain dreams. Plans remain on the drawing board. Spiritual potential is never realized. Goals are unfulfilled. Life becomes unproductive. Mediocrity spreads throughout the Body.

When the Bible speaks of self-control it uses a term that literally means "to be inwardly strong." Another meaning is "the ability to submit." Self-control is the ability to say No to the lesser and Yes to the greater. Throughout this chapter the terms self-discipline and self-control are used interchangeably, because both refer to inner strength and the ability to put aside the lesser for the greater.

Paul provided two illustrations of self-control. He was able to face many problems in life because he focused his attention on the *eternal* rather than the *temporal* aspects of life. "For momentary, light affliction is producing for us an eternal weight of glory far beyond all comparison, while we look not at the things which are seen, but at the things which are not seen; for the things that are seen are temporal, but the things which are not seen are eternal" (2 Corinthians 4:17, 18).

In another passage Paul emphasized the necessity of spiritual discipline in contrast to bodily exercise. "Discipline yourself for the purpose of godliness; for bodily discipline is only of little profit, but godliness is profitable for all things, since it holds promise for the present life and also for the life to come" (1 Timothy 4:7, 8).

Bodily exercise is profitable; I find it helps me function more efficiently. But if I spend all my time exercising my body to the exclusion of exercising my soul, I will lose both in this life and the life to come. "For we have brought nothing into the world, so we cannot take anything out of it either" (1 Timothy 6:7).

DISCIPLINE FROM NATURAL RESOURCES

Some individuals seem naturally to have greater self-discipline than others. Studies reveal that certain personality traits are blessed with this quality. In his book, *Spirit-Controlled Temperament* (Wheaton, Illinois: Tyndale House Publishers, 1966), Tim LaHaye writes, "*Mr. Choleric* is usually a self-disciplined individual with a strong tendency toward self-determination ... Once having embarked upon a project he has a tenacious ability that keeps him doggedly driving in one direction" (p. 26). And, "A melancholy person can always be depended upon to finish his job in the prescribed time or to carry his end of the load" (p. 28).

Others have received excellent training in their homes. As children observe disciplined parents, they tend to follow that example. But in homes where Dad spends his evenings in front of the tube and Mom allows the house to look like a disaster area, the children have another pattern to carry into their own marriages.

Many have benefited from early religious and moral training in their homes. They've learned the difference between right and wrong. They've developed a sensitive conscience. They've learned to resist many temptations in life because they know the consequences. Such individuals may have no relationship to

Jesus Christ, but through religious and moral training they've learned to say No to certain types of sin.

Some children have learned about hard work because they've grown up on a farm. Others have received their training through a background of poverty. While going to school they worked after school hours. This routine was carried on through high school, perhaps even college, and today they are disciplined self-starters.

DISCIPLINE FROM A SUPERNATURAL RESOURCE

If some "natural men" (without Christ) are disciplined in life, how much more we Christians, whatever our personality or background, should be. We believers have access to a supernatural resource. "For God has not given us a spirit of timidity, but of power and love and *discipline*" (2 Timothy 1:7). The Scriptures expand this concept: "But the fruit of the Spirit is ... self-control" (Galatians 5:22, 23). The potential for discipline or self-control is within you if God's Spirit is within you (Romans 8:9).

You might not possess a personality that lends itself naturally to self-discipline, but you can possess the Holy Spirit. Your background might not have been one that set a good example of self-control, but if God's Spirit indwells you, discipline is at your fingertips.

GREASED POLES

Climbing a pole is difficult, but if the pole is greased, the task is almost impossible. Some of us are attempting to climb greased poles as we struggle toward self-discipline.

One of our problems is *lack of goals*. This was my own problem up to my second year of college. I didn't have the foggiest idea where I was headed in life. I had no reason to study. I barely made it through high school, and when I arrived on the college campus (thanks to an uncle who was the football coach), I carried my haphazard study habits with me. Though I tried to be a better student, I had difficulty with follow-through. I was distracted by anything and everything. At the end of my freshman year I was placed on academic probation.

During the following summer I was determined to join the Air Force, much to my parents' dismay. I went down to the recruiting office, but as I was about to enter, I had second thoughts and postponed my decision.

Near the end of that summer, God broke through to me. There were no bells ringing or trumpet blasts, but the still, small voice of God's Spirit impressed me to prepare for a life of ministry. It was difficult to explain to friends and relatives, but my parents understood that God's hand was upon me. I now had a purpose in life, I had goals, and I was determined that by the grace of God, I'd learn to study and become the best student I could. Though I never became a straight-A student, God enabled me to maintain a strong B average throughout college and seminary. Self-discipline wasn't an automatic experience. But as I kept my eyes on my goals, I developed a life of academic discipline that has become an invaluable asset for my pastoral and writing ministries.

Paul recognized the value of goals for a disciplined life. "Do you not know that those who run in a race all run, but only one receives the prize? Run in such a way that you may win. And everyone who competes in the games exercises self-control in all things. They do it to receive a perishable wreath, but we an imperishable" (1 Corinthians 9:24, 25).

Another "greased pole" is *lack of commitment.* We refuse to pay the price for excellence. We love pleasure more than productive work. The twelve-year-old boy learns that it's more enjoyable to play baseball with his friends than to practice the piano, and unless his parents intervene, his interest in piano will fall by the wayside.

The adult who values security over a productive life will find it difficult to be an individual. He will become a man-pleaser. He will say Yes to various requests in spite of his qualifications. Whether it takes him from something important or not, he volunteers, hoping to be accepted by his peer group. Much of his time is spent in nonessentials. Active? Yes. Productive? No.

Another greased pole keeping us from a disciplined life is our *dependence upon feelings*. A student tells himself, "Tonight I'm going to study." But as evening arrives and he takes a stab at the books he concludes, "I just don't feel like studying. I'll try tomorrow night."

As I look back on the writing of this book I can honestly say that of these chapters, I *felt* like writing only two or three at most. Sometimes the inspiration was there, but most of the time neither inspiration nor feelings overpowered me. I wrote anyway, because the book would never be completed if I waited to feel like writing.

Where does the Holy Spirit fit into the picture? Lack of goals and commitment and dependency on feelings don't sound too spiritually oriented. Oh, but they are! We must first understand the various goals which the Lord gives us. Next we commit ourselves to them and walk by faith rather than feeling.

One such revealed goal, for instance, is given in Colossians 1:10: "...to please Him in all respects." I have a choice. I can commit my life to pleasing either myself or God. As I allow the Holy Spirit to control my life, I develop an increasing desire to please him in all respects. According to the same passage I can please God in two ways: "bearing fruit in every good work and increasing in the knowledge of God."

When I allow God's Spirit to control my feelings, he empowers me to fulfill worthwhile objectives in spite of how I feel. He may not change my feelings, but he will discipline me to act in faith: "Lord, I believe this is what you want accomplished. Therefore I'm available to fulfill your will."

DEVELOPING SELF-DISCIPLINE

But to be more specific, consider self-discipline as it affects six areas: our bodies, minds, time, finances, sexual lives, and tongue.

Self-discipline needs to be applied to the *body*. It baffles me how some Christians can get worked up over smoking and drinking, while they carry around fifty to a hundred more pounds than needed. And much too often, the man behind the pulpit becomes the greatest offender. The Bible declares that our bodies belong to God (1 Corinthians 6:19). We don't have the right to do with them whatever we please. To neglect exercise, overeat, and get too little sleep is to insult God. The body is an instrument of God, a temple of God, designed to glorify God (1 Corinthians 6:20).

Bodily exercise may not be as profitable as the exercise of the soul, but it is still worthwhile. Of course we all don't need the same amount of exercise. A farmer won't need as much exercise as a pastor. He gets enough exercise with his daily chores.

Another way to discipline the body is to make certain it gets proper rest. "It is vain for you to rise up early, to retire late, to eat the bread of painful labors, for He gives to His beloved even in his sleep" (Psalm 127:2). Discipline may cost you the late movie on TV. It may mean cutting down on night meetings. But it will be worth the price.

A third way to discipline the body is to eat sensibly. This means the right amount as well as nutritional balance. The individual who goes without breakfast and then stuffs himself with rolls at ten A.M. and desserts at lunch is hurting himself.

Weight gain and loss are so logical that we often miss the essential principle of proper maintenance. All things being equal, we reap what we sow. If we put 3,500 calories into our bodies, but burn up only 2,500 calories, we have a problem. If we put 2,000 calories into our bodies and burn 2,500 calories, we experience weight loss. If we want to maintain proper balance, we must learn what we are able to consume without gaining and then stay at that level of intake.

A further way to control the body is to change pace periodically. This may include a vacation, a day off, or a weekend retreat. Some men boast, "I never take a vacation. I don't need it." Eventually their widows disagree.

Is it God's will for us to have bodily discipline? Definitely (1 Corinthians 6:19, 20; 9:24-27). We can therefore commit ourselves by faith to this biblical goal, asking God's Spirit to empower us with his discipline, even when we don't feel like it.

The *mind* must also be disciplined. In some Christian circles, ignorance is equated with spirituality. Education is seen as Satan's tool to destroy spiritual growth. It never occurs to some that education can be God's tool to develop maturity in a believer.

True, Peter and John weren't the intellectuals of their day (Acts 4:13). God blessed them as they reached out to the common man, but whom did God choose to reach the philosophers of the first century? The man who was well trained in the Law of the Jews and the wisdom of the Greeks. And even though that wisdom was foolishness to God, the Apostle Paul could gain a respectable hearing and preach the wisdom of God (Acts 17:16-34).

But disciplining the mind isn't limited to formal education. Many adults have become avid learners after they've finished formal education. Some develop their minds by reading. If a person reads good books, he expands his perspective on life. How tragic that so few people read.

Others spend time thinking (the Bible often refers to meditating). Speaking of the productive individual, the psalmist wrote, "But his delight is in the law of the Lord, and in His law he meditates day and night" (Psalm 1:2). Today we hear about meditation in the Eastern religions and the cults. Satan has gotten his people to meditate day and night on man's wisdom, while many of God's people meditate on the talk shows at night and the soap operas by day.

Other means of disciplining the mind include listening to cassette tapes, participating in Bible studies and discussion groups, attending adult education opportunities, and conversing with others.

Peter says, "But sanctify Christ as Lord in your hearts, always being ready to make a defense to every one who asks you to give an account for the hope that is in you, yet with gentleness and reverence" (1 Peter 3:15).

Have you ever witnessed about Christ to someone who asked you questions for which you had no answer? You walked away licking your wounds. You felt foolish because you didn't know what to say. But then you determined to get into the Word. Praise

God for opportunities that drive you back into the Scriptures, disciplining your mind.

Discipline is also essential in our *time management.* The Bible tells us to redeem the time (Ephesians 5:16, KJV). This means we should make the most of it. Two excellent books on time management are *Managing Your Time* by Ted W. Engstrom and Alex MacKenzie (Grand Rapids, Michigan: Zondervan Publishing House, 1968) and *Tools for Time Management* by Edward R. Dayton (Grand Rapids, Michigan: Zondervan Publishing House, 1974).

We must also discipline ourselves in *money management.* We usually conclude that our financial problems are the result of not having enough money. Actually that is probably only a symptom of a greater problem: mismanagement of what money we have. Madison Avenue spends millions of dollars to teach you poor management of your finances. Without the discipline of the Holy Spirit you're destined to become just another consumer statistic. What does the Spirit teach?

He first informs us that we are stewards (managers) of God's money rather than owners of our own money. God gives us money. "But you shall remember the Lord your God, for it is He who is giving you power to make wealth" (Deuteronomy 8:18). "Furthermore, as for every man to whom God has given riches and wealth, He has also empowered him to eat from them and to receive his reward and rejoice in his labor; this is the gift of God" (Ecclesiastes 5:19).

God also has power to remove our financial security. "You have sown much, but harvest little; you eat, but there is not enough to be satisfied; you drink, but there is not enough to become drunk; you put on clothing, but no one is warm enough; and he who earns, earns wages to put into a purse with holes ... Why? ... I called for a drought on the land, on the mountains, on the grain, on the new wine, on the oil, on what the ground produces, on men, on cattle, and on all the labor of your hands" (Haggai 1:6-11).

Once we understand that our money (like our bodies) is not ours to do with as we please, we will recognize the importance of proper management. The Holy Spirit informs us that God must be placed first as we begin to distribute our paycheck (Matthew 6:33). Too often we reverse the order. Uncle Sam is first, and the bill collectors. Then come our desires (our desires often precede our bills, resulting in more bills). Then with whatever is left (usually very little), God is tipped on Sunday.

Many Christians think they can get away with this. "Will a man rob God? Yet you are robbing Me! But you say, 'How have we robbed Thee?' In tithes and contributions. You are cursed with a curse, for you are robbing Me, the whole nation of you! Bring the whole tithe into the storehouse, so that there may be food in My house, and test Me now in this, says the Lord of hosts, if I will not open for you the windows of heaven, and pour out for you a blessing until there is no more need. Then I will rebuke the devourer for you, so that it may not destroy the fruits of the ground; nor will your vine in the field cast its grapes, says the Lord of hosts" (Malachi 3:8-11).

Put God first, pay your bills, save some of your money, and spend what is left for necessities. Then watch God prove his promise and supply your needs (Philippians 4:19). "And God is able to make all grace abound to you, that always having all sufficiency in everything, you may have an abundance *for every good deed* ... Now He who supplies seed to the sower and bread for food, *will supply and multiply your seed for sowing* and increase the harvest of your righteousness; you will be enriched in everything *for all liberality*" (2 Corinthians 9:8-11).

Besides self-control in the use of our bodies, minds, time, and finances, we are to be disciplined in our *sexual lives* (1 Corinthians 7:9). We are constantly being bombarded by society's standards and Satan's lie: "indulge now." But the devil is the father of lies and doesn't deliver what he promises. Instead of joy there is sorrow. Instead of security there is loneliness. Rather than a sense of success there is failure. In place of freedom, one experiences guilt and slavery.

The Spirit of God provides two ways in which we can achieve greater discipline in our sexual lives. First there are several preventive means. The Bible tells us to abstain from every form of evil (1 Thessalonians 5:22). Don't read *Playboy* or *Oui,* even if your friends tease you. Give up sensual novels, R-rated films, sexually stimulating clothes, and anything else that leads you into temptation. An alcoholic attempting to break his habit would be foolish to spend time looking at ads that entice him to drink. We're just as foolish if we think that sexual trash is harmless.

What if you suddenly discover yourself in an awkward situation? You hadn't planned on it, but there you are, caught in an extremely tempting circumstance. The Holy Spirit has an answer for that situation: "Flee youthful lust" (2 Timothy 2:22).

Young Joseph found himself in just such a situation. He was quite handsome (Genesis 39:6) and very appealing to the king's wife, who plotted to entice him into immorality. He refused, but she persisted. Then one day when no one was around she actually grabbed Joseph by his clothes and pleaded, "Lie with me!" Joseph didn't stop to argue. He knew that reasoning was out of the question. He turned and ran out of the room as fast as he could (Genesis 39:7-12).

Another way by which we can prevent loss of sexual self-control is to stay in the Word and maintain a dynamic relationship with Jesus. "How can a young man keep his way pure? By keeping it according to Thy word. With all my heart I have sought Thee; do not let me wander from Thy commandments. Thy word I have treasured in my heart, that I may not sin against Thee" (Psalm 119:9-11). If all your time in school is taken up with academics and social life, your resistance to moral temptation will be greatly weakened. Get active in a local church or campus ministry. Maintain private devotional life with the Lord, and he will empower you to resist the lust of the flesh.

But what if I've already blown it? Is there any hope for me? I've been unfaithful to God. I've defrauded my girlfriend, or I've given in to my boyfriend. Where do I go from here?

God also gives us a corrective means to develop a disciplined moral life. It begins with confession. The word *confess* means that I say the same thing God says about immorality. "It is sin." Don't call it a mistake or a weakness. Call it a sin.

But confession goes further than that. Some believers confess sin as though they were reciting the Preamble to the Constitution. They mouth the words, but they don't mean what they say. Their confession is as profitable as if they'd rubbed a rabbit's foot twice for each sin committed. Confession must come from the heart as well as the mouth.

Confession also includes one other aspect. Sometimes we confess sin at one moment and justify it at the next. "Lord, I confess that what I did was wrong. I acknowledge it as sin. But you know I would never have yielded, if Jim hadn't lied about his love for me." When David confessed his sin to God, he didn't blame Bathsheba for taking a bath out on the roof top. He said, "Wash me thoroughly from *my* iniquity, and cleanse me from *my* sin. For I know *my* transgressions, and *my* sin is ever before me. Against Thee, Thee only, *I* have sinned, and done what is evil in Thy sight" (Psalm 51:2-4).

Once we've confessed our sin we should claim God's forgiveness. You can do this by thanking him that he has forgiven you completely. Thank him that he will never hold you accountable for that sin. Then, give the control of your sex life over to God's Holy Spirit. Allow him to empower you and break any immoral habit you've developed. Keep walking by the Spirit's control and he promises you that fleshly desires will not be fulfilled (Galatians 5:16).

Finally, we need to experience self-control in the *use of our tongues*. James wrote, "But no one can tame the tongue; it is a restless evil and full of deadly poison" (James 3:8). We can negatively affect a child for life with a scathing remark about his appearance or ability. We can ruin an honest man's reputation by passing on a false rumor about him. We can quench great potential in a growing youth by informing him that he'll never amount to anything.

Careless and bitter words are destroyers. Jesus warned, "And I say to you, that every careless word that men shall speak, they shall render account for it in the day of judgment. For by your words you shall be justified, and by your words you shall be condemned" (Matthew 12:36, 37). How can God justify or condemn someone on the basis of his words? Jesus said that a man's heart is exposed by his lips. *"For the mouth speaks out of that which fills the heart"* (Matthew 12:34).

When one person orally assassinates another, he informs you

more about himself than about the person he is attacking. He exposes his own bitterness, jealousy, or possibly his ignorance of the facts.

No one can tame the tongue, but God's Spirit can. We therefore have a twofold responsibility: (1) to commit our tongue to God, and (2) to turn away from using our tongue for evil.

God is willing to take what we give him. He receives our anxieties (1 Peter 5:7), our praise (2 Corinthians 9:11, 12), our finances (Malachi 3:10, 11), and our bodies (Romans 12:1, 2). He also accepts the control of our tongues. "Let the words of my mouth and the meditation of my heart be acceptable in Thy sight, O Lord, my rock and my redeemer." "Set a guard, O Lord, over my mouth; keep watch over the door of my lips." "O Lord, open my lips, that my mouth may declare Thy praise" (Psalm 19:14; 141:3; 51:15). Turning to God with our tongues will enable us to turn our tongues from evil (1 Peter 3:10).

Determination is not enough. How often have you had to confess, "I don't understand what made me say that. I had it all worked out beforehand. I knew what I was going to say. I promised myself I wouldn't get angry. But when I began to speak, it just came out."

Because the tongue exposes the heart, you and I must begin with the heart. When the Holy Spirit is allowed to control the heart, the lips will show who is in control. When God reigns in our hearts we will speak words of encouragement (Ephesians 4:29-32), words of thankfulness (Ephesians 5:4), and words of praise (Ephesians 5:19, 20). But when the old self is behind the steering wheel, look out—deceit (Romans 3:13), cursing (Romans 3:14), criticism (Philippians 2:14), malice (1 Peter 2:1), and filthy talk (Ephesians 5:4).

An athlete, a fine musician, a good student, or a successful businessman doesn't "just happen." These individuals are what they've become through self-discipline. Likewise, a well-balanced, mature believer doesn't just happen. He runs the race according to the rules. He wins the prize because many times along the way he learned to say No to lesser things, that he might attain greater things for God.

If Jesus Christ is your personal Savior, you have all the potential discipline and self-control you'll ever need for successful living. How? By also having within you the spirit of self-control in the person of God's Holy Spirit. So run, that you might win (1 Corinthians 9:24).

spiritual transformation

One of the most frustrating tasks for parents is teaching their children the need to change clothes. Boys are usually slower to learn it than girls. The typical grade-school boy would wear the same underwear, socks, and dirty jeans for weeks, if his parents didn't intervene.

When sinners become Christians, they receive a new spiritual wardrobe from their heavenly Father (Luke 15:22-24; 2 Corinthians 5:17). But many seem satisfied to walk around in their old clothes in spite of the dirt and grime. They have to be reminded time and again to get rid of the old clothes and put on the new attire God has provided.

Paul writes, "Away then with sinful, earthly things; deaden the evil desires lurking within you; have nothing to do with sexual sin, impurity, lust and shameful desires; don't worship the good things of life, for that is idolatry ... You used to do them when your life was still part of this world; but now is the time to *cast off and throw away all these rotten garments* of anger, hatred, cursing, and dirty language" (Colossians 3:5, 7, TLB). "Now your attitudes and thoughts must all be constantly changing for the better. Yes, you must be a new and different person, holy and good. *Clothe yourself with this new nature*" (Ephesians 4:23, TLB).

But where do you start? Many times you've tried to be like Christ. You've wanted to experience love, joy, peace, and the other qualities of the Spirit's character. But you soon found yourself wearing the same old clothes of anger, bitterness, envy, jealousy, lust, etc. Why the problem?

MISPLACED DEPENDENCE

In your attempt to become more Christlike you may have depended on things that were never designed to produce spiritual character. Take *self-development programs* as an example. You can learn how to become a better salesman, a more effective leader, or a positive thinker. You can experience various improvements in your life. But to identify such improvements with spiritual growth is to fall short of the goal. Friendliness, better organization, and optimism are a definite advantage, but life can continue to be filled with anger, jealousy, hatred, and lust. The only good result is that others don't have to put up with so much. You learn to cover up your real self and put on a smiling mask.

Another area of misplaced dependence is a *special spiritual experience*. Some believers experience glossolalia (speaking in an unknown tongue). They may view this incident as a certain sign of Christlikeness. But the Corinthians used tongues and were still carnal. Other believers may experience a special healing in their bodies and link the event with great personal faith. But when you read the account of Peter's healing the lame man at the gate of the temple, there is no evidence of faith on the man's part. His mind was set on receiving money, not healing. "And he began to give them his attention, expecting to receive something from them" (Acts 3:5). Even Peter, James, and John had quite a spiritual experience up in the mountain where Jesus was transfigured before their eyes. There, standing a few feet from them, were Moses and Elijah. Added to these extraordinary visual phenomena was an audible voice: "This is My Son, My Chosen One; listen to Him!" (Luke 9:35). But did these experiences make Peter, James, and John greater spiritual characters? A few sentences later, Luke wrote, "And an argument arose among them as to which of them might be the greatest" (Luke 9:46).

Think of the nation Israel. They saw the pillar of fire leading them at night and the cloud leading them during the day. They witnessed the parting of the Red Sea and crossed it on dry ground. They ate the manna and the quail. Their clothes lasted for forty years (Deuteronomy 29:5). But the nation worshiped other gods. They were immoral and rebellious in spite of their great experiences.

A significant spiritual experience may impress upon us that God is alive and powerful. It may be the catalyst that causes us to hunger after him. But we cannot depend upon past experiences to make us spiritually mature.

Another temptation is to depend upon *past success.* Gain a victory over some problem area of life,and what happens when you face a similar problem again? You're tempted to think, "No problem. I've handled worse situations before. I'm building up an immunity to this temptation. I've really matured." Result? Timber-r-r-r! "Therefore let him who thinks he stands take heed lest he fall" (1 Corinthians 10:12).

A fourth area of misplaced dependence is in *our spiritual gifts.* When I wrote *Discover Your Spiritual Gift and Use It,* I had hoped readers would experience drastic spiritual changes. They would develop a greater love for others. A sensitivity to the Holy Spirit would grow. Patience and gentleness would characterize their lives. But I have reservations now. I've met too many highly gifted individuals who use their God-given abilities to advance an ego trip. Their motives are questionable. The results of their ministry are exaggerated. Personal spiritual character does not govern the use of their spiritual gifts. Satan is pleased.

Spiritual growth may be initiated or encouraged by self-development programs, spiritual experiences, past successes, and spiritual gifts. But none of these in themselves is the source of spiritual character. God is. He alone can begin, continue, and complete the task of character development in our lives. Jesus said, "Yes, I am the Vine; you are the branches. Whoever lives in me and I in him shall produce a large crop of fruit. For apart from me you can't do a thing" (John 15:5, TLB).

Jesus' promise is that fruitfulness is a direct result of abiding in Christ. Spiritual character is developed in proportion to the relationship we maintain with our Lord.

ELEMENTS ESSENTIAL TO CHANGE

The first question that I would ask someone having a difficult time in his spiritual life is, "Do you really want to change?" Change must begin with *desire*.

I've discovered in my counseling that the average troubled person has a strong desire for a more meaningful life. He doesn't want the guilt feelings, hostility, and tension he experiences. When I share the process he must go through, however, to make that bountiful life his own, the desire may quickly fade.

We live in a society that has bought the "something for nothing" philosophy. Workers demand more pay for less hours. Many aren't well qualified to handle the jobs they are given. In order to hold their jobs it is no longer necessary to become more efficient or more productive. There is really no need to improve at all. Your security comes from seniority or tenure.

The Scriptures offer a more realistic philosophy. "He who sows sparingly shall also reap sparingly; and he who sows bountifully shall also reap bountifully" (2 Corinthians 9:6). In other words, if we put little effort into a changed life, we shouldn't be surprised when little change takes place. Do you really want to change? Do you want it so much that you're willing to do whatever is necessary?

Once an individual is ready to make this type of commitment, he is ready to include the element of *evaluation* into his program for developing spiritual character. Which of the fruits of the Spirit do I most lack? Perhaps the previous chapters have helped you perceive both strong and weak areas of your character.

Vulnerability is another element in the process of change. When I was a boy we used to play baseball in the streets of Lancaster, Pennsylvania. At the end of each block there were storm sewers. It wasn't unusual for one of us to hit a fly ball that sailed over an outfielder's head, rolled down to the end of the block, and went plunk into the storm sewer. The water level was normally about five to eight feet below the street. Since we never had an abundance of baseballs we made every effort to retrieve the ball. The usual system was to connect two of the tallest and strongest boys to the smallest. Each of the tall boys would take a leg of the little guy and put him headfirst into the sewer. Usually I was unanimously nominated to brave the stench, gook, and threat of extinction. I was vulnerable.

God doesn't often ask us to volunteer for sewer duty, but he does ask us to become vulnerable to him. He wants us to place our ambitions, plans, hopes, fears, in his hands. You may call this attitude trust or faith. What name we give it is of little importance. What is essential is a total sellout to the will of God.

A fourth ingredient of spiritual character-building is *exercise*. "But solid food is for the mature, who because of practice have their senses trained to discern good and evil" (Hebrews 5:14).

A number of years ago I took a speed reading course. I had hoped that by attending the sessions faithfully and taking good notes I would increase my speed ten times. At the first session the instructor informed us that we would have to read one hour minimum each day. We would have to move our fingers over a page even if we missed many of the words. She said, "You're going to be tempted to give up. You'll get discouraged. You'll convince yourself that this is a lot of nonsense. But keep practicing, keep reading, follow the instruction, and I can guarantee a marked improvement. Fail to practice and I can guarantee nothing." She was right. I experienced all the temptations our instructor predicted. Every other day I was ready to throw in the towel. But in spite of my mixed feelings, I continued to practice. The results amazed me.

As you begin to apply the various principles of this book to your life you will be tempted to give up. Satan will attempt to convince you that your old habits and attitudes aren't bad enough to warrant such drastic action. He'll tell you that you're as good as most Christians. He'll suggest taking a break to spend some time in front of the TV or read a risqué novel. He may get you caught up in a lot of religious activity so you have no time to exercise spiritually.

Temptations will confront you. But in spite of how good the "easy" way looks, "discipline [exercise] yourself for the purpose of godliness" (1 Timothy 4:7). "And let us not get tired of doing what is right, for after a while we will reap a harvest of blessing if we don't get discouraged and give up" (Galatians 6:9, TLB).

Another element needed to develop spiritual character is *perspective*. When we develop an inward look, we may keep gazing at our inadequacies and become discouraged, or keep gloating over our strengths and successes and become proud.

God is the supply source for every blessing, spiritual or material. Paul wrote, ''We dare to say these good things about ourselves only because of our great trust in God through Christ, that he will help us to be true to what we say, and not because we think we can do anything of lasting value by ourselves. Our only power and success comes from God'' (2 Corinthians 3:4, 5, TLB).

There have been times when I felt inadequate to express Christian love to certain individuals. But when I took my eyes off my insufficiency and focused on God's ability to love, I experienced what I couldn't produce myself: a deep unconditional love. Many times I've felt inadequate as I've worked on sermons, counseled the disturbed, and prayed with the hurting. But whenever I turn the problem over to my supply source, he comes through.

Desire, evaluation, vulnerability, spiritual exercise, and perspective were not always part of my personal life. I was always more of a *do-er* than a *be-er*. My emphasis has usually been on abilities rather than on character.

CONFESSIONS OF A PREACHER

Somewhere I read that there are three kinds of people in the world: (1) those who watch things happen, (2) those who make things happen, (3) those who don't know what in the world is happening. I determined that I would belong to the second group. I wanted to make things happen. I put this desire to work in my first pastorate.

I began my adventure by setting long- and short-range goals. I knew where I was going and how I would get there. I got others to work toward my goals. In order to guarantee success I asked God to bless my efforts. He understood my immaturity. He was patient with my slow learning. Excitement, growth, involvement, increased giving were part of God's blessing. I was learning how to preach, administrate, listen, teach, and counsel. The people were responsive.

I felt, however, that something was wrong. I was letting the people down. I had taken them as far as I had gone with the Lord myself. I didn't know where else to go. People were discovering their gifts and using them in the church. I personally was using all that I thought God had given me. But something was still missing. I wanted a deeper life for my people and myself, but I had nothing to offer.

I concluded that the people needed a new pastor who could take them into areas of the Christian life that they'd never seen before. I needed a new challenge to stretch my imagination and faith, to shake loose the spiritual cobwebs I'd gathered over the years. I brought the matter before the Lord daily.

Several months later God made it clear that he wanted me in Fresno, California. Through a series of circumstances, encounters with various people, and an open door in Fresno, the decision was made.

First came the honeymoon stage. Again I set my goals after making several surface observations. But, like the experience President Ford faced when he pardoned Nixon, I began to recognize early in the "Yohn administration" that the honeymoon was over. An opposition party began to form—and as it grew, my own hostility developed. I soon realized that I was becoming something other than Christlike. I resented the fact that people weren't recognizing the need to make changes in their lives. I didn't appreciate their lack of faith in my leadership.

Nearing the end of my first year in Fresno, I had become frustrated and confused. Where was I going? What should I be doing? Why couldn't I get rid of these resentful feelings against people?

The answers began to express themselves loud and clear. "Rick, your focus is wrong. You want people to respect your leadership because you've experienced a successful ministry in your former pastorate. You can provide them with better organization, innovative programs, and more personal involvement. But you won't take these people any further spiritually than you led your other congregation. Your spiritual gifts have their limitations. Your education can provide the people only with greater knowledge, and knowledge can lead them into spiritual pride (1 Corinthians 8:1). Your people are divided. They need to love and be loved. They need to care for one another. They need to feel free to share their burdens and blessings. You aren't helping them because you haven't come to this spiritual level in your own life. Like pastor, like people. Let me begin to bring a character change in you. Then you'll witness spiritual growth in your congregation.''

My prayer life took on a new dimension. ''Lord, begin to make the necessary changes in my life. Remove my bitterness. Cleanse me from resentment. Every time I look back at past success, remind me to thank you for producing it. Guard me against depending on my gifts, education, or experience to accomplish what you alone can fulfill. Create in me the burning desire to be like your Son Jesus. And Lord, allow my people to see what you are doing with me, so that they'll desire the same for themselves. May our congregation become known for our walk by faith and love for one another.''

As the days passed I learned to say with Paul, ''Now glory be to God who by his mighty power at work within us is able to do far more than we would ever dare to ask or even dream of— infinitely beyond our highest prayers, desires, thoughts, or hopes'' (Ephesians 3:20, TLB).

PROVISIONS OF A LOVING FATHER

The Lord first began with spiritual renewal in my own life. He made some significant *attitude changes*. He helped me understand that most of the people with whom I had difficulty were merely reflecting my attitude toward them. I began to see them as brothers and sisters in Christ who needed love rather than criticism. I also started to realize that I could learn about myself from even the most obnoxious individual (who exposed areas of my life that needed improvement).

My attitude toward problems took a turn for the better. I usually looked at problems as obstacles to success. They were annoying, frustrating. But now I'm coming to accept problems as opportunities for God to demonstrate his power and wisdom. I'm beginning to understand James' perspective. "Dear brothers, is your life full of difficulties and temptations? Then be happy, for when the way is rough, your patience has a chance to grow. So let it grow, and don't try to squirm out of your problems. For when your patience is finally in full bloom, then you will be ready for anything, strong in character, full and complete" (James 1:2-4, TLB).

I also saw myself in a different light. No longer did I have to prove myself. I was convinced that my responsibility was to walk humbly before God (Micah 6:8). I would constantly seek his direction for the life of my congregation. I would become more sensitive to the needs of my people without conforming to every whim and fancy someone might have. And whatever I did, my ambition would be to bring praise to my Father in heaven.

Besides the attitude changes, the Lord produced renewal as he began to reveal *new truth* from his Word. The Scriptures became living and powerful. Rather than look at God's Word as so much information to impart, I saw it as life-changing truth that had to be shared with others. Much of my preaching had previously been directed to people's minds. Now the appeal was directed toward their hearts and wills. I became convinced that they had problems and God had solutions.

A third area of change had to do with organization and program. Earlier, everything I did was predetermined in my study. I established goals. I developed plans. I followed schedules with precision. I greeted any interruption or failure with hostility.

Today I continue to set goals, inaugurate programs, and follow schedules. But the Lord has added a new ingredient: *flexibility*. Two principles have led me to accept flexibility. From the realm of experience I've learned that "whatever can go wrong will go wrong" (Murphy's Law). This meant that no matter how well I planned, there was no guarantee that performance would be flawless.

Another principle that helped me with flexibility was the proverb, "The mind of man plans his way, but the Lord directs his steps" (Proverbs 16:9). I realized that in spite of right motives and the best plans I might develop, I couldn't know all the facts. The margin for human error was too great to think I could meet all needs all the time. Therefore, I now make my plans seeking God's wisdom. Then I place them before him. I ask the Lord to make all necessary changes before or during the time they're implemented. And as he makes the changes I'm learning to accept the finished product as his will.

A fourth provision from my heavenly Father was a *new awareness* that God is the source of life. I had often confused bearing fruit with producing fruit. A grape branch bears grapes, but it's the vine that produces the fruit. Jesus said, "I am the vine, you are the branches" (John 15:5). For many years I thought I was responsible to produce top quality results in my ministry. Therefore, when the results were significant, I could pride myself on a job well done. But if the results were insignificant I became depressed and frustrated.

Today I can thank God for the privilege of ministering as faithfully as I know how. Now I allow him to produce the results of his choosing. As in agriculture there are seasons for sowing and reaping, so in serving God there are times I sow and another reaps. At other times I reap what another has sown (John 4:37, 38).

Recently we had a well-known speaker in our church. He was an effective communicator. God blessed his ministry and many people responded to his invitation. Someone wondered how I felt when I saw more people respond to him in one day than to my ministry in a year. I replied that I was delighted. The sower and the reaper rejoiced together because both realized that it was God's harvest.

Because God is the source of life I can count on him to produce the results of his choosing in his time. I am learning to relax in the Spirit. I study, prepare my heart and mind, and communicate the Word of God to others as effectively as I know how. Then I thank God for any result he chooses to produce.

Freedom to be myself in Christ is one further blessing. For quite a long period I would observe others in my particular area of service. I attempted to discover what made them successful so that I could pattern my life after theirs, and of course I would become frustrated. But the Lord opened my eyes to see that his special plan for me differed from his purpose for others. He gave me willingness to accept what I couldn't change and determination to improve what could be improved. He encouraged me to focus my attention more on spiritual character and less on spiritual gifts. As long as I thought about gifts, I considered what I was doing for God. But as I directed my attention to character, I could concentrate on what the Lord was doing for me. The former focus led to pride, the latter to praise.

God may not produce the same changes in your life, because you may not be so deficient in spiritual character as I. But there is always room for improvement. Our spiritual gifts are not enough. The Lord will make us effective Christlike believers as we allow him to develop our spiritual character.